COMRADE PAST & MISTER PRESENT

# ANDREI CODRESCU

## New Poems & a Journal

# COMRADE PAST
# & MISTER PRESENT

COFFEE HOUSE PRESS :: MINNEAPOLIS :: 1986

*Dear Masoch* appeared in OINK! 18 (Chicago), *The Fourth of July* was in NEW DIRECTIONS 48 (New York), *Music* in SMOKE SIGNALS (New York), *When Lightning Struck, I & II*, in CHANNELS (San Francisco), *Momentary Bafflement with Return Home at Dawn* in UNMUZZLED OX (New York), *Rejection* in REJECTION (Oakland; it was specifically written for the first and, alas, last issue), *Blues for Casanova* in HOT WATER REVIEW (Philadelphia), *Co-here Britannia* in OARS (Cambridge), *Petite Madeleine* in OPEN 24 HOURS (Baltimore), *Comrade Past & Mister Present* in SULFUR (Los Angeles). *The Juniata Diary* was published in UNITED ARTISTS (New York), HOT WATER REVIEW (Philadelphia), SMOKE SIGNALS (New York)

The publishers thank the National Endowment for the Arts, a federal agency, for a Small Press Assistance Grant that aided in the production of this book.

Cover by Claudia Tantillo

Frontispiece by Alice Codrescu

Coffee House Press books are available to the trade from Bookpeople, Bookslinger, Publishers Group West, Inland Book Company, and Small Press Distribution. They can also be ordered directly from the publisher. For orders, catalog, or other information, write to Coffee House Press, Box 10870, Minneapolis, MN 55440.

Library of Congress Cataloging-in-Publication Data

Codrescu, Andrei, 1946-
      Comrade Past & Mister Present.
      I. Title
PS3553.03C6      1986            811'.54            86-2681
ISBN 0-918273-21-8 (pbk.)

# Contents

# COMRADE PAST & MISTER PRESENT

# DEAR MASOCH

Dear Masoch doodling with his contracts
pens Venus in Furs on the margin of the document
he is preparing where it says
how many lashes he must receive, and where,
when the door opens & in the gaping doorway
a head framed by Viennese blue says:

"I am a Girl in Search of an Interpretation
filled with creamy snow like a vanilla éclair
I am waiting in the window of the dusty
European Poetry Shop for a soldier
to bring the following question before us:

'What do you do if you're a masochist but have been placed
in a position of power?'"

The girl who is the skinny international type
as yet unknown for another century
but whose prototype is already visible
in certain forward-looking writers like Madame de Staël
who is taking the species from courtesanship
to traveler's checks
hides behind dark glasses and travels with only a toothbrush
and a diaphragm in her straw bag,
objects unknown as well although their prototypes
in the form of rough twigs smeared with dental powder
and sea sponges soaked in torn anemones
have been in Masoch's house before.

She has power over boys and is equally at home with money.
He says:

"You must use your power to draw contracts specifying the amount
of prose I mean pain you want inflicted on yourself."

She is leaning on a cardboard structure waiting
for him to take her photograph and to sever the strings
by which the large balloon tied to the structure
is lightly attached and when sufficiently airborne
to take hold of her feet and kiss them.
The life of her soles flickers briefly above him
like the life of dreams flickers above all tales
& glows after they are told, for a second.
Her entire world is covered with graffiti. They say
Read Me. Interpret Me. He will. He does. He lifts the glass
paperweight holding down the poem and out the window
it flutters. Her damp pulse is in evolutionary
overdrive.
"They imagine they think," she says.
"I can get around reason as easily as Nietzsche
gets around his house to meet his fate. Or face,
as my mother says. 'You must have face!' 'With
face all things are possible!' If action is
the unreasoned interpretation of my position
whose oddity is beginning to bother me, then we are all
in the interpretation business. The reasoned
readings should, according to the interests
of the reader, be either weighed down or inevi-
table, so either let go of my foot or cut the strings."

It is a moment filled for Masoch with the rapture
of understanding nothing. Therefore he leans on the
poetic misappropriation of his youth by certain
aborted flights of reactionary romanticism
and pours out of himself:

"Oh, but I want to be thin and filled

with your doomed elegance like *filet de* swan, like
old verse in the corrupted daycore…fancy
the daycore when I am through with you!"

The barely heard music of the threat is not lost
on the aspiring masochist. She too
is leaning on an obsolete tradition
instead of going to law school:

"A man furnishes his heart with explanations.
There, the chair. That's where the mirror goes."

"In a cheap hotel."

"So cheap I dread to think of the knives glinting
from the unbuckled belts of torn'd pants — men lurking
in the dim one-watt light bulb halls soggy
with blood their carpets still fresh from recent
beatings and forced strippings
the doors impossible to latch the windows painted shut
with an intoxicating lead-based paint
the bed sheets — what is left of them! — displaying
maps of *terræ incognitæ* in sperm and constellations
in blood drawn by either lice or the monthlies of
street women or forcibly taken virgins
and the constant hum! the screaming of busted
water pipes the moans of the dying junkie next door
the impossible visions of the nymphomaniac drinking in
three burly men at once, a fight on the street.
And then I see the terror on your face as you lie
under me being ridden like a nasty nag to your doom:
'What is the matter, scum?' I ask and follow
your terror-crazed eyes to the ceiling where they rest
on a monstrous *fleur-du-mal* painted on the ceiling
with human blood and brains. It appears

3

that someone lying on this very bed
put a gun under their chin or in their mouth
and decorated the ceiling thus. 'Oh!' and I can
feel it, the elusive gift of total surrender
as two prongs like a snail's horns shoot out of my
clitoris and antennalike begin to pick up the beat
from the far-off galaxy where I really live."

"And then just as my terror is transformed as well
into the pleasure of having fulfilled my contract…"

Masoch waves the contract in the air.

"You get up pull up your little flowered undies
and leave, slamming the door behind you so that
a few chips of ceiling blood flake over me like snow
and I must stay there, like that, egglike
for at least fifty years until psychoanalysis
becomes a respectable profession and a psycho-
analyst a person one can call from a hotel
in the middle of the night, even in Marseilles."

"In all this," she says separately, to someone apart,
"Reason looms separate and voluntary like a fruit
in a rabbinical garden, or braces on the teeth
of Mormon belles. We are none too sure if the
Mongolians we imitate know how to read, and I don't
like yogurt. And I assume that reading,"

she turns the page

"is all there is, even if I'm awake. Especially
then. Can fresh water make it seem like next day?
I know who's listening and I came too soon.
The holes in space are purring like a cat, calling
attention to their idealism or their exactness

4

They don't breathe too hard, or too slow, they are
not in a hurry, there is a universe next door,
a reversible fragment. Refreshed, after she slept,
Reason awoke to find Goya's monsters perfectly
appropriate, artistically drawn, and all that,
and in her mental baggage. Get those things out
of here! she cries. I will not rest until I make
an aphorism as good as those they have assigned
to me, and on she goes, I mean on I go, insisting
on the right to a nearly empty straw bag over
my shoulder, and a passport. I tell you, the original
mistake of philosophers is to keep silent
on music and on cars."

Misguided Masoch holds the trembling rifle he's been
holding for an hour, hoping to shoot Karl Marx. From
the dusty hideout in the fork of a twisted olive above
a farmer's pigsty, he calls to the thin shadow slowly
going from him like an effete oxcart:
"Untranslatable you! Banal futurism! Our paper servers
are combing the future for you! You are hardly
capable of understanding anything except your little
beastie-in-residence! You have been infected by the
legalization of pain and are no more than a bored fire
burning itself out in the bush alone, without a city,
firemen, great engines, excitement, and the press. The
overstimulated mind elite of which I was once part
is no more. We have taken to the twisted branches
of the olives with rifles. There is action in us! Oh
yeah! There is a kind of sleep in us from which
you will be born. I love you."

There is a brief report. A dove with a bullet in her
beak flies away. The two WWs in the form of two fat crows
stand on the branch above Masoch and chatter in frigid

5

vulgate. A caterpillar which is actually a grenade pin
pulls himself slowly out, and the explosion is loud
enough to eliminate the peasantry and rearrange the
geodemographics of the world. Of course, none of this
bothers Masoch. His name is immortal, and the contracts
he has drawn standard. The striped fields cross
the sentence in the hand-held word-mixer searching
like floodlights for the skinny psychopath from another
century who stands in her kitchen under a meteorite
shower mixing herself a Margarita. The urgency holds
her breath as she passes from the gates of metaphor
to the little Formica table where the sun shines
so lovely in the a.m. There is a chipped vase with
field flowers in it, some wilting, and a handful
of scallions rising next to it like the African
proletariat which never panned out. Deadjectified
she leans limply on the sill of her youth. She could
zip up her parka & mount the demented tractor still
and consider the transmission and love, which is
a motor function, but it is too late. The revolution
has subdivided her into dumber & dumber characters
like a trompe-l'oeil landscape composed of zillions
of theories, which she could think of as either
grist for the mill, or angels. In either case she
is a boss and an employer. Her passport has been
canceled, she can drink her drink overtly for the use
of money, or covertly for the repopulation
of the planet with tiny insectlike machine people
forcibly pulled out of the planetary psyche
which, empty, reels like a great revolver chamber
filled with the souls' ungraspable trajectories,
or she could *in extremis* call for her flesh
and for the bitter conclusion of her contract
with Masoch, which is death.

"None of that," she calls from the doorway
under the blossoming arbor where she has set
up an alternative to the hotel rooms of Marseilles.
"No dread sobriety should attend the gestures
of those present, no one should signal intently
to something out of sight, there will be no taxi
obscured by a tree with the motor running. No
furrowed brows ploughed under by thought, no
pajamas. No obvious seeds sprouting discreet
flowers, no discreet flowers at all. Only grotesque
flowers like one-eyed Susans, the floral Cyclopes. No
gents with violets, only gentians with mimosas. Only
uncertain professions, no new branches of mental
hygiene. No sulphur baths, no inception of chills, no
thermometers. No chilly languages, no translations
from chilly texts. No translators catching colds
from opening windows between languages, no crossroads,
only real stammerings, true hollows where the tongues
stand in their cases heavy with the awkward honey
of the first spoken, the as-yet-unsaid, the moist
dimensions, childhoods with animals, childhoods
that are great battles not preventive thoughts,
there on streets that can't exist, igniting
themselves with food mass-produced from all the nos
& no-nos a woman & her dummy can attract in a long
& unruly life, a river of charm, really."

Her voice runs from her like a monk pursued
by a buggering papyrus. Why are we not
in this book? cry her lovers. Because, she says,
without this time opening her chapped quotation
marks, those I love quietly do not textify
as readily as those who cause disturbances,
men like Masoch here, and other literary figures
whose photos I collect. All these guys do is

talk poems with big P as if the A-bomb wasn't
capital enough. Guided by styles, imagined
buildings, things impossible to draw, idiot
fantasies, wallowing in the rejecta of their
childhoods, they have originally happened
to someone else. To me they are semaphorisms,
crustaceans renegotiating the order of isms,
who have died for something in the future, some-
thing Sundaylike but juicy, the skin of something
basic and direct, why beat around the bush: me.
What good is the good horseman after he lost
his head? Plenty, say I, both the crazed horse
and the head that goes on thinking, rolling
crazed eyes at the border guard who wants to see
inside. They all want to see inside, it becomes
necessary to see inside every minute, then every
second it becomes necessary to see what's new,
or if the old is quaint yet, or if the dream
of lit has added anything since the oral rap
of certain marsupials. The fear is always
that we might go away before we figured out
why we came in the first place. That we might
run out of text in the flower of our youth,
not like Keats running out of youth in the flower
of his text. That we would crouch behind an unrehearsed
bit of prose, ready to pounce on the slightest
poem biking by, only to find that sentences
stretch into years, that years flow into pages,
that the world gets erased as quickly as we type,
that no one types, that a large gaze holds us
transfixed in its unblinking, flat look. You
really want me to put you in this book?

Having taken full advantage of her escape
from quotes, she stretches under the waterfall

8

of Masoch's steady penmanship under a backdrop
of Toledo swords and hears the pirouetting
of her shadow in his sleep, a sound like that
of a young Arab crouching behind a garage.

What legal needs I have, spoke Masoch from his branch,
which, used with the one below, served him
for the quotation marks he too had just escaped,
have been vastly rankled by the future
which responds only to forced entry and is
always the enterer, not the entree. Therefore
I'll charge myself a fee for every error of fact
and give myself a whipping for every odd fancy.
The State is a terminal cancer, it sucks
the lollipops of our souls, it sits on our skulls.
She does not exist.

Oh, but I do.

# THE FOURTH OF JULY

I know a sad and large man who lives in West Germany.

That's how I thought I would start a newspaper article about a man I don't know, a Romanian poet who sends me his sad self-published little books every three months or so. This man is a doctor, a G.P. probably in a small coal-mining German town. I see the post office where he buys his stamps and gets his mail and the little coffee shop where he has his *schwarz Kaffee* and writes his sad poems. His poems aren't just sad, they are desolate, they are haunted, they are hollow and ground-down, the despair is thick and incontrovertible. There are leaden seas and hopeless rivers in them and burnt trees with dots of pain on the charred branches. The humans are missing from his landscapes as resolutely as if they'd been rubbed out so long ago nobody even remembers them. But once in a while a remarkable little human thought will make its appearance, astonishing in its petty incomprehension. Things like: "They've thought of it, so now I have to eat it." Does he have a wife, children? Probably.

Today is the Fourth of July. The radio plays the "Ode to Anacreon," from which F. S. Key took "The Star-Spangled Banner." I'm an American, no doubt about it. My heart swells with pride at this brass riot, I am transported. I love Mr. Jefferson. A genius. A revolutionary. A great visionary. He would have puked on Ronald Reagan. He would have put little Ronnie on one of his enormous, historical knees and puked the remains of an immense vegetarian meal washed down with grog on Ronnie's little head. Ronnie should be so lucky!

Whenever I go into a school, I try to get maximum erotic charge from youth, so I compose odes which correct the obvious inconvenience of actual bodies and their deformities.

only rarely among youth, in schools, do you actually *see* a shining body or mind. You just suspect that they are there, because they *have* to be. So sayeth all of folklore. So sayeth your old mind. So you bring out these things that all these things sayeth by means of odes.

> Always use their typewriters
> They will never be the same
> Stoned keys the silent arbiters
> Of dangers hidden in a name.
>
> Not that the poem comes out best
> In jail, but under the piano or
> In the dusty street where the rest
> Roll back eggs into the nest
>
> Of a fact in the sidebar of a news-
> Letter being put together by young
> Bodies complicated not obtuse
> Transparent, sincere, oh skinny tang!

How silly. But you can bring out youth by these semihermetic means, if only because curiosity makes a creature bloom. But I'm not even being amused. I simply suffer the ignominy of cuteness, the futility of pretending something for a bit, a tiny bit of money. Meanwhile, the children, the bodies I am teaching, are immensely rich. Half the children are millionaires themselves, the other half's parents are. There are Mercedes, Cadillacs, Jaguars parked in the school lot. You can hear a kind of contented gurgle, the flowing of milk through the well-worn channels of oligarchic tranquillity. There are names here that go back to the founding days of the Republic, traditions tighter than a harness on a cavalry horse. The military, business, and managerial castes have money riding on these children. Indeed, they ride *on* money, like wagons on rails. The youth I am trying to bring out is the youth that is being ground out of them by means of a rigorous education. The forms of youth are set, the manifestations coded, the clothes prescribed, the limits defined. I'm a fool, in the English office, with an old typewriter.

I can imagine this little West German doctor, this terrible poet, this sad caricature in Germany, the Germany of the post-post-miracle. The burghers are only now awakening from the post-war miracle, and they find themselves to be little Americans! Cubed houses, disposable cars, fast food! But they are only formally Americans, Americans without Mr. Jefferson. Inside, they are nobody. At the center of the nobodyness of their hollow insides sits this sweating little immigrant, this sloppy fat doctor writing his desolate, horrid, hopelessness-filled works. He is like a wafting of bombed basement, this little foreigner, his dark eyes darting between one hollow breast to another of the mastectomized owner of the little café where he likes his *schwarz Kaffee* hot. He knows that her breasts are only rubber balloons: he ordered them for her by mail, and he adjusts them every month.

The radio hostess was so-o-o thrilled to have me on her show. It was like having a doll or a new dress, something so-o-o exciting! I had it in my mind to make her laugh. It was, ultimately, too easy. She was already laughing when I went in. She laughed all the way through the introduction, then laughed at her own question, then literally *cracked up* – her make-up opened up like an earthquake into myriad gray lines – and she *kept* cracking up. It was epic, completely out of proportion with what I heard myself saying, which was nothing. "Read to me," she said, "something from your pockets." I'd just told her that my pockets were filled with art, notes, poems, that they were veritable mines full of treasures, all one had to do was dig, dig. I put my hands into the left mine, pushed past

South Africans with headlights, and pulled this out and read:

"All have secrets who have experienced inexpressible things. A secret is what has no language. Morons have the most secrets. The NSA and the CIA, which have the most secrets, are the world's biggest morons. After that come poets, who are forever struggling with the inexpressible and are only capable of small portions of it, meagre meals to be sure."

"Oh! Oh! That's so-o-o! Read it again, please!"

I read:

"Everything is inexpressible. Morons are walking bombs bursting with secrets. We sat down at a meal of filet moron and were quickly imbued with mystery, soaked in essence, perforated by the elsewhere."

Behind the twinkling eyes of the radio hostess, the automatic question-making machine broke down, and for a moment the wires showed. Through the cracks in her make-up I saw someone squatting on the ground in August, making peepee, while enormous black clouds covered the earth. Soon it was going to rain.

Kansas is as big as the world.

Either I have been blessed with content or cursed with it. Whichever way you look at it, it's work. Without content it's easier work, dependent on other means of support, some of them truly undignified. With content it's a mixture of work and some of the easiness of non-content. The payoff of content is fame, money, immortality, a seat at the circus.

Like flowers growing out of thin air, or enormous vegetables in outer space, with their roots showing like the obscene nerves of molars, the little West German exile's poems grow and scintillate with a life of their own, nourished by a deep fake memory, no talent and no music, in and of themselves like Leibniz's spheres. He admires their growth, despises himself, bows to the other customers. It's closing time at the sad café in the sad little provincial town in little America Germany. Everyone now must go home to their cement cubes to turn on the TV. The proprietess thrusts her rubber balloons provocatively forward as she wipes the spot of dry *schwarz Kaffee* on the marble top. With a sudden gesture the poet sticks his fork into one of them. It deflates with a sad hiss, letting out sad years of marital juggling, pastel dreams, a variety of mouths stuck at various angles of greed, their teeth shining and showing, and air. "*Oh, mein Gott!*" mumbles the terrified poet. "Frau Goebbels! I didn't mean to!" He takes his poor head between his sweaty, trembling palms and, with a resolute gesture, pulls it off his neck and, in the same movement, lifts the blouse of the proprietess and sticks it in there where the deflated breast can be heard breathing its last pfffssst! It is, needless to say, a huge head, completely out of proportion with the other rubber breast, giving her, momentarily, a grotesque appearance. It has all happened so fast! Frau Goebbels is so astonished, she has not stopped wiping the spot of *schwarz Kaffee* on the marble top. But it's a fact: the head of the poet is now the left breast of the café owner. And there is terrible disproportion between left and right, a kind of monstrous political imbalance possible only in Germany.

I meet a friend of mine for coffee downtown. This friend of mine is a poet who has been in school for a very long time. He has a degree in poetry. He writes a very precise kind of poetry that is very much like the poetry other school poets write. His poetry is very comical, actually, but he thinks of it as at least profound, if not tragic. He is all worked up over a parable he has found in a story by Borges, a parable that concerns him personally.

It appears that a king had commissioned a poetic battle from a poet. The poet came back with a great poem full of great poetic victories. The king gave him a mirror, told him to go away. Ten years later, the poet returns with the battle. He reads it to the king, and it *is* the battle. The king gives him a gold mask. The poet goes away for another ten years, whispers something in the king's ear, and kills himself. The king gives up kinging, becomes a beggar and wanders about in rags.

"And," my friend said, "I'm now working to become perfect at the battle, so I could get the mask!"

I felt suddenly very sorry for him. All that schooling wasted. All that dedication coming to naught.

"Listen," I said, "that mask is only a medal of service. The poet had only managed to return the mirror to the king so the king could see himself. So he gave him a medal of service to the state because he'd finally learned how to politick and flatter. Alas, the poet was only a poet when he brought in the first poem. After that, he was only a courtier and a vassal."

"How about the last part?" the poet protested vehemently. "Isn't the king wise to give up? And isn't the poet wise?"

"That last part is disgusting," I said. "Of course, old men become wise. What else can they become with a foot, a hand, and a tongue in the grave? Still, the poet is wiser than the king because he has the good sense to go in search of the unknown. The king just walks around hoping to hear from the dead, which is probably what the poet promised him, that he would come back in another ten years with the news, if not a new poem. And the fool king believes him."

"That's terrible," the poet says. "Do you want to talk about something else?"

Never. I never want to talk. I throw the waitress an evil look and leave.

The proprietess, left hanging there with uneven breasts, faced the West German without a head, trying in vain to look into his eyes. She would have done better to lift her blouse and look into his eyes there. But then a miracle happened. The head began to shrink. No, the other breast began to grow.

No, the head began to shrink. No. And so on. I could care less.

A sudden rain is going to drown out the fireworks at the harbor. But the radio goes on, playing my song.

*July 4,* 1983
*For Ted Berrigan*

# MUSIC

There were no bums in my pores.
New York had opened my pores & bedenimed & bendovered
    walked in my fantasies
        shoving bums.
The stores were open and the hours late.
Expectations were being fed
        not sent to work
        like in far-away San Francisco.
I could speed up & slow down
    grimace & guffaw
        move my hands
          & look up to the lit windows
filled with admiration for the natives
    though not wanting to be asked in
since my living room at the moment was the biggest.
I was digging the streets & the streets dug me.
Every lunatic sped toward its co-lunatic.
Bellevue was lit up like another apartment building
    & in fact a party of sorts was going on
      with the inmates happy to be warm
        even as they were being hurt.
Ambulances piled in front & people went in & a few
        came out
    & the enormous hallways could have fit
      a Communist city's living rooms
        which they did
because on several floors the inmates slept there
but these hallways were dirty green & bright yellow
    & the neon was dirty
      & the unhappy floors
were track-marked by wheelchairs & police boots
        & mad jigs

& flares & broken glass.
The floor to be sure was a picture of hell.
The prison ward was behind two tall gates &
    wire-mesh windows
        an easy jail break
& the cops were half cops & half social workers
    & in go the two poet workers
            with their two culture cops, i.e., books
    & there are the prisoners
        half wanting to look at a woman
            & half desirous to look at free folk
    & half sick of each other
        & half sick
    & half serious criminals
        wanting to improve their lot in life
    & half mad criminals
        who had it in for the other half.
One came with a bed and a trapeze for his bandaged arm
        & half a body in a cast
    & another walked in wheeling a tall steel cane
on a flying saucer from which flew an IV bag connected
            to his arm
        & as he walked
        he recited bathroom walls
but was interrupted in midrhyme
        by an atmosphere of human color
            occasioned mostly by a reader of best-sellers
            who wanted to write them
because he had lived dramatically & was interested
    in technique & his interest
        led to metaphysical questions
            which gave the poets a license to interrupt.
Another was grim & tall & black
        & in his head he carried
the entire philosophy of an obscure mystical sect

in severe couplets:
"In the middle of the pyramid there is an eye.
The dollar bill has a lookout in the fourth sky.
The steps to the Capitol are seventy-three.
That is the number to cross the zebra & the flea."
   I am probably being unjust
     to a grim mystical doctrine
       which the man whispered
         before being led out
           by Big Sister
             in midrhyme.
It was an evening to forget & one to remember.
It was 9:45 & the night was young.
At 10:25 I had collected myself sufficiently to return
  to the world hopeful
    & why not
when so many were rhyming the world in their heads
    even on their back & in bandages
& while you can't call this feeling love
    there being no room for close-up oppression
there was a hope that half was not lost.
Parts of the Sunday newspapers still covered the city.
The stores were open & a thousand ways to get high too.
Denizens of the night revealed fragments of wild costumes.
In the bookstores an intellectual orgy raged.
The smell of pastry & coffee was being attacked by ginger
      & Mongolian pepper
        from inside red restaurants.
It was possible to consume everything or nothing.
Either way the balance was righted
  the consumers as passionate as the ascetics.
The Lower East Side of New York
    moved eternally by a rhythm
  "beating outside ordinary time"
      no shit

the graces of cheapness.
Cheap were the pirogis
   at the Kiev.
Cheap pirogis at the Kiev
   6 boiled with sour cream $1.95
a whole subclass converted to Ukrainian food
   & this without pamphlets
      or monks,
each pirogi a pamphlet-monk
   doing its preaching in the mouth:
"if the Ukraine is ever to be free
   you must eat all your pirogi"
though there are people who do not like them
because they have first seen them fried
which is not always the best way to make somebody's acquaintance
not a pamphlet-monk's certainly
   & halfway through my second pirogi
   the radio said John Lennon was shot.
John Lennon was shot by an assassin.
Minutes later the radio said he was critically wounded.
And later yet that he was dead.
   The waiter held his plates in abeyance
   & his face became very sad
   & a tear fell on a pirogi
   & I was still hopeful but shocked.
A man named Chapman meaning chap man man man anyman
   "I am no man"
   a failed double with a gun
   a fallen half
had been shooting at a symbol & killed Lennon instead.
And now his music came from the sidewalks
   & everyone understood
   & became much sadder
   & their tears fell
on solid gold pirogis rolling into image-making machines.

The symbolists had killed John Lennon
    & I thought
    look at it as a vacancy
    a power vacuum
    a king is dead
    it will make everyone think
    for a few seconds before commerce sets in
       & that's no way to think
         but it was thinking me.
Chapman was now in Bellevue where I had been
       11:15 p.m. Monday, December 8
  an hour earlier
  with the other halved halves
& the hairs on my arm stood over the pirogis
    when I remembered that it was here
      in the Kiev
        ten years ago
          that I'd heard of Bobby Kennedy's death
which at the time struck me like the free winds of doom
    with the apocalyptic illumination
      of anarchist Jew
        I owe to myself.
Ah cheap pirogis in love with yourselves!
I was in love but with no one in particular.

*Dec. 22, 1980*

# When Lightning Struck, I

*After* The Pit, *by F. Norris*

Genius
totality under partial control
a corner of the Market
part-time demiurgy

Then the waves come
and bury him in wheat

he couldn't rise to the job
when the earth took him seriously

Minutes later only a finger still shows
pointing to the clock
then it too goes under
a wave that feeds half of Europe
and drives a wedge between the American farmer
and his radio

He should have followed rhythms
not newspapers
though briefly they coincided
to do & undo him

Toward him comes the female of the species
and together they billow to California

to fight for a sincere blue reflection

# WHEN LIGHTNING STRUCK, II
*Petit Eros and J. P. Morgan*

A little frigidity allows the mind in
A crack in the door
With mind comes a new kind of money
*Soma spermica* the unspendable
Funny money between each other's legs
Buttery beast music issuing from the earth
All the heroes get knocked up by their heroes
An imperative stands on the end of the nineteenth century
Like angels on the tips of all those erections
Everything is urgent cruel and industrial
Sweat wheels turn about the shoulders of modern girls
Lightning is a basic sentence the night is a book
Not yet remaindered the avantgarde steps forward
A clamor for the moon overtakes the desire for saints
Movie stars purchase all the existing halos
Haley Muller Herschel Menelaus Nectaris Somniorum Tranquillitas
And sex is Muzak in Selena's mart J. P. owns
*Homo sapiens* turns into *Homo interruptus* WW I
Machines outdo themselves break down and weep
The hardwon hardons enter the Catholic lotteries
Genitalia swim & splash in the light of their own fantasia
The light comes on in the great white suburbs
To calypso beat of nymphomaniac drinking chemicals
The guy in op-art pajamas Mr. Morgan
Stands on the military lawn under a December moon
Of the next century          Behind him the door is cracked
In front of him two Frenchmen keep digging into the asterisks
Which are actually millions of people dressed by record companies
And pull out clouds of untranslatable bullion
Someone help me it's freezing out here he says.
He pukes out his gold libido egg.

23

Beginning in his tiniest earliest first person singular
A music advances into his hearing until he can't believe his ears
The acoustics of royal capital grow
Loading him with multicolored firecrackers
He swells to range over the Indian and Pacific Oceans
Impossible to pursue except by large generosity
Is lost for a few minutes in the equatorial belt
Which henceforth is destined to replace his pajama string
A rainbow for scarf      Infinity before and after
And is so vast finally he leaves the sentence
Bequeathing the earth to the smokestacks of his factories

# Momentary Bafflement with Return Home at Dawn

Extremely logical circumstances are in effect:
we are in danger of behaving as expected (though
how to create a red rage or what anyone expects
and where...) I feel
most strange: could someone have taught me an iron-
clad logic while I was sleeping at Carmen's house?
Oh, Christ, push the furs aside
and ask to see the Furrier! Sir, do you know
anything about this? I was coming home appalled at the
submivissness
submissiveness
of lawns and yet I could not start
a revolution among the worms. It was
strange indeed to find my madness lacking militancy.
I am not, Sir, pleased. I would like my perceptions
to march on the capital! Un-
fortunately I cannot appeal to other madmen: we
are all mad in different ways and the wonderfully
sane masses will never hear this pitch: they are
boarding the buses for work.
Everywhere they are boarding the buses to work.
The right to insist must be natural.
If they are, I will too. Sleeping securely
when everyone is gone is a luxury for that; I think
my body is made of a soft alloy of dead cats and lead
and folded to requirements.
I wouldn't mind auditioning for the Night
just as long as I don't get a part. Just for the
experience. I have a bad memory,
it's possible that I already have. In fact,
I remember: there was this river
in the middle of which a rapid and deep hole beckoned.

in the middle of which a rapid and deep hole beckoned.
Out of it a fish came:
Audition in ten minutes! he told
a number of bathers of which I was one.
And surely, soon we drowned.
They looked me over: not enough dark meat for the Night!
Try the Day!
Ah, well, I surfaced with a new view
of things in which order was not essential,
greed even less so.
Of course, I can't be sure that secretly
the director adored me or not, I tell
a number of café regulars of which you are one,
but one never knows for sure if *mission* isn't really
an issue.
So there, have a cigarette.
In the Cavity at the heart of this matter
things are occurring I wouldn't to any recommend,
things both disgusting and completely eerie.
There is a law I imagine, carved on the walls the way
the Communists carve little heads of Lenin, the way
life is carved on palms for all to see,
but what this law purports to regulate is well
beyond me. The question is:
can one ask the driver midway down the precipice at the
foot of which a ten-foot spike looms, if he could
please turn around and sign here?
Or the glove out of control, inside the vagina, provoking
the race to a duel, if it would please return
to the hand it fell from when it slapped the Intruder?
Now or never, one would like to say, tomorrow
they close the post offices.
Yes, but we will still have bath-
rooms and handcuffs! Chairs and gladiolas!
A different species inhabits the laboratories!

The joy is so great one would like to shout goodbye to
every one of one's sperms: 20,000,000,000 goodbyes!
Once in a while one makes it to my eyes.
I couldn't make it in the outside world, honest.
The space would render me catatonic, soon they would
have to pack me against the wall under a lantern
with a bunch of souls sad indeed.
I'm getting off the bus: they have something missing
in their gait, something
props them up, lighting matches
after orgasms.

# Blues for Casanova

The room was filled with black boxes.
There were no children anywhere.
There were six of us stuffing red gloves
and black stockings inside.

Then Daddy came in and said:
Clean up your room. The King is coming
for dinner.

The King enjoyed very much pulling
things out of black boxes.
He called this "dinner."

When the Revolution comes no one
will do this any longer.
There will be no more grace left.

# COHERE BRITANNIA

parallel coherent worlds       tectonic plates
jam and push up
that's no mountain that's the wedge of a perfectly coherent
world pushing up through this one like china through down-
town san francisco in the form of the transamerica pyramid
this sudden person under the window not there when i last
turned an intentional gaze into coherent scan is the advance
solo flag of a self-contained nation we know nothing of

suddenness is the signal of coherence incognito
subsumed by the typing hand which when withdrawn retires to
a place full of hands manuela tends
ditto the head
in the headarium subdivision is the full-time activity
time being in charge of its own linear coherence in charge as
well of what it contains conceiving it
never a dull moment

coherence in its own bag is being home
coherence in a double bag at the supermarket is being in prison
you boys better cohere here by the window
a coherent view of the yard leads to a better and more coherent
vision of things to come in a fine coherent world
cells cohere
coheres *ceolli mundum*

lemme give you the coherent version of our position several
years ago me and a country i've never been in meshed whereby
i cohered into a society of former strangers and was reduced
to coherency not to speak tears having to constantly enforce my
and their coherency with clichés i got so much shit together it
uncohere my anus to reflect the universe was one all this time

a one i held on to dug and grooved with all the coherence at my
side a sort of gilded lance and me saint coherence all set to
leap on two three four five and so on whenever things got nasty
in fact they were nasty one out of two fact being coherent by
virtue of corroboration
fact as coherence model
they had seventeen witnesses escapees from the local nut house
and one official in charge of capturing them who saw nothing
*nota bene* in the presence of any coherence please check to see
who is in charge then draw a map of the facts as you see them
facts tend to unsheet

all things become incoherent when incapable of defending them-
selves with maps i.e. unsheeted facts
coherence equals attention span
absorbed by a fly birds become incoherent to the ornithologist
the assumed coherence of the religious-minded young larry z.
makes everything everything and since he has no attention span
we wish him good luck in the hands of his faith
because he will have none at my hands which are now typing him
out larry who
all the coherence aphorism lent the world was lost when the
aphorist became a sonneteer
when god has logorrhea someone has to invent the haiku
a violet
blooms in his skull
the first flower of Spring

# Petite Madeleine

We never discuss tenancy
We are a most peculiar couple
Our street isn't on the map

I remember kissing you
Form is punishment
The being compelled to it

Pays in full for the sizzling
Neuron grid clamped tight
On the cracked map

If you do what you think
You have to you can modernize
Yourself all on your own

Cooked in the end by micro-
Waves sweet fleeing monk
Buggered by papyrus

With first act of play on it
Performed by ancient photog-
Raphers in the loud mud

Of Egypt Mesopotamia Babylon
Dacia Illyria Thrace Baton Rouge
Mass-produced blow job's

First Henry Ford a cosmopolitan
Criminal in Communist journalism
Walking to and fro in the glass

Aquarium of agents in the know
This street can't exist
So let's do it again

Doubling the windows and the bricks
Turning the vibrant hermeneut
Loose on the twelve-story building

Each story a bit peculiar
Self-told but totally dependent
On its mad teller's psycho-

Analysis like an I-told-you-so
Told in a thousand languages
A million inflections

Still what was it I told you
In the first place second third
I kissed you you had your orders

# VOLCANIC DIRGE & CO.
*For E. B.*

My life is all made into lit
Like some kind of raw material for export.
Until now "I" had controlling interest
Having nationalized the self for which
The only demand came from the forging of a taste.
Others could mine what they could use for spice.
And now you come along and corner the depressed
Market like Bunker Hunt.
You're welcome.
Loquacious before history
But speechless before talent.

That's understanding so I understand.

## En Passant

Having avantbiographed the world
To make another come right out of it
I have certain scribbler's rights
On the next one – endlessly impregnate
The self about to be designed.

I praise the lava holes

whence issued my first passport.

## THE INNER SOURCE

All good things
    eggs & hashish
come from Molotov's eye
    & return to Stalin's.
What I'd like to see
      he said
is a poem without Stalin.
    Me too.
There are certain kinds of typewriters
made for Ted Berrigan staccato poems –
    especially elucidating the question
of audience as singular.
         The same machine
addressing itself abstractly to a theme
    or a plural audience (also theme)
      would be more of a machine,
i.e., would be more æsthetic.
    Addressed
      to you
        it wobbles
betwixt the listening to itself & the void.
Likewise the telephone, said F. O'H., and true.
One gets his effects, said Lenin,
    from speaking to all as if all were one,
      thereby birthing the Hell's Angels.
But Stalin said
    entering the poem through the back
      that one must speak to No One
        as if all were included.
It never occurred to Homer to include No One
    though he invoked his guises.
And F. O'H. took to eliminating No One from the address

by putting a name in the blank,
an intelligent listening.
A great deal of whistling wind between a civilized
address in a city with streets
& a steppe with hosemen picking teeth with lances.
Conquests instead of dentists
oneness instead of arthritis.
Detritus humanists stash egg in the aortas.
A word sucked from the air and lightning
spewed smoking out into the mouths
of a million baby birds
versus
the word ESPRESSO in neon and the rain
beckoning anonymously warm in Paris, France.
The verbiage of frozen butts upon the saddle of loud death
sugar crystallized above the hush
of cottony May evening *sur le coin
de table.*
History of what rounds (how many)
and what babble
before specific address
and hey, hey, that was me talking
to you walking

away.
Go on
while you still can
before they notice.
It is in this way
that the listener departed
a long time ago
from an address in the city
changing his number leaving no telltale traces
or tales.
The one Mongolian who tried was turned
into thin slices and worn under the saddle

36

till pastramied.
The N.Y. Deli on Second proudly serves him now on rye.
Consequently only good Mongolians tell long tales.
The epic-homosexual tradition
survives intact
in the unaddressed
without address
but tightly
packed.
The anonymous alienated prosaic use the full-page bourgeois
indigested aspirined and hebdo dramadaire Cointreau's sex
sated deconstructed (self) lophe
tell toted (melted)
on the spot
where addressed
where the telephone
was.
Imagine Stalin phoning up his troops one by one.
Imagine Mayakovski phoning up his fans one by one.
Imagine Dylan Thomas remembering each girl he fucked.
Imagine Whitman remembering each blade of grass.
Imagine Stalin phoning Mayakovski.
Imagine Stalin phoning Frank.
You can't imagine that?
Frank phoning Stalin?
Of course.
Let's talk mustache.
Let's hash the hush.

# NOVEMBER 6, 1984
*For R. K. on Rereaganization*

History's can
                     can only be filled
by brash moves
               not memory's trash.
He whipped his thigh as he spoke
               straightened out his tie
checked the spokes of his auto.
           History can only be
           produced as a design.
           In history people are
           elements of design.
           The hero whips in to
           restore the order.
           The world's a mess.
On Tuesday at 1:15 more or less.
     The heads pop. This evening
at precisely eight o'clock
Reagan's wrinkles will envelop the nation.
Anarchy's about to break loose. The made-up
President steps in
               his dummy walks out.
       A simian, somatic metaphor, whipped
           sleep, Apollonian zero,
               full can.

# School Daze

Topaz extra: that's *stoned*
    Missed it in all the talk of ropes
        & animals.
Stoned among ropes and animals, wrote Ovid,
    get me outta here.
Those ropes and animals turned out to be my country
      for a few hundred years. Liked esp.:
    the cow, goats and sheep,
        and the poets, the flute players.
In the halls the flute players hold pencils.
They draw breasts with them all over the papers.
        Teacher, Teacher, what did I get?
        An A Breast, my pet.
Oooga! There is a tit on my test!
A toast to your tit! And so,
        he continued,
a city that isn't sexy is like ropes lying there
    in the old Black Sea port
after all the longshoremen died of clap
& the dusty statue of Ovid applauds all by itself,
some Roman joke floating in from the Turkish coast.
But look, what's that? A cargo ship filled with
intellectual Nubians holding books by Susan Sontag...
    It can't be true: that's a flotilla
with all of New York aboard, including but not
confined to criminals, psychpats (that's pats
    you get in psych class), lunch-counter lizards,
  bus-stop toothpick types, bag ladies, cops, and bugs.
They are coming here to get out of New York.
They are going to disembark in New Orleans
        and continue on foot to Baton Rouge
where they'll become Ovids (a brand

of cigarettes).
So pass the horizontal days atop the tilted nights.
Eight days later
Time's house goes Bye

# COMRADE PAST & MISTER PRESENT

Can the misfortune of a dog owned by vegetarians
be felt by a woolen creature exuding class privilege?
Looking through windows to glimpse tits I saw this
instead. It wasn't in the manual. But
applying private cures to collective diseases
occupied every page, it was *The Book of
the Transparent Tombstone.* You could see
all the heroes inside, and downtown Chicago,
men like Mr. Wrigley and buildings like the Tribune
Tower, and what they felt being there like that,
men and buildings squashed inside the look
of a drunk poet chased by wind
like a Sunday supplement on Monday morn.
You could read their desires but not their thoughts,
because you can read those like cigarettes in Lebanon
or Madagascar, and they said,
The thing to be is dead. Complete
thought evacuation. The cold wind
said that. The buildings themselves said
other things, having to do with stubbornness,
heart, commerce, stability, the will
of large men who know the world well
enough to sell it, and when.
You cannot throw up a building in Chicago,
my friend Debra says, and what, say I,
do I look big enough to throw up buildings?
Maybe my steak, but not a whole edifice, no.
You cannot, she says, do that unless it says
something, and buildings in Chicago say
some pretty strange things these days. I look.
They do. They say,
Choke, choke, have another drag,

then take a piss, warm water from the womb,
before starting to fire those tiny letters again.
A deaf woman with sign-language cards lurches
past a horn of plenty filled with writhing pretzels.
The deaf don't get fed here.
Not here now, a waiter tells her, and Gertrude echoes
from the wall:
There is no now now.
In France the dead gods were replaced by waiters
from many parts of the world, many grand waiters, former
czars and dukes and interior ministers
whose manners struck terror into the diners' hearts
and caused a form of socialism whose central burning
question was How do we put the pleasure back in the food?
I call the woman back and say, Ten cards! I have ten
nephews who need to speak your language. They live
in France. They operate a great Deaf Restaurant
where one day the cook chopped a customer's arm off!
On the same spot, a hundred years before
they guillotined a count under the eyes of his pastry
chef! And right now, at this very moment, as I sign,
the half-guillotined bourgeois extends
the stump of his patriotic arm to the former Bulgarian ambassador
(one of the cousins I just mentioned,
also a former Communist and member of the police,
but now a maitre d' and cook, and, secretly, a poet)
who holds it in the air above the slowly turning
rotisserie of history and orates thus:

At the present I cannot address my sentiments to the public,
because they will laugh at them, so I say to myself,
Scribble, scribble in the night, poet.
You are the sole mumbling interpreter of
an older art lost to the anxiety of the milieu,
a man from history, a faucet and a book, in a position

to know and to tell that
culture heroes are not characters, only private heroes are.
And you know also what's inside buildings people don't
really live in, in a country without directories.
But telling the truth after so many years of partisanship
is something I, the ambassador, cannot face.
But a roast, ah, that is incipience *and* fountain!

A very poetic busboy, a cousin I don't remember, streams
out of the kitchen sink
and cuts into the wounded grand bourgeois
and former commissar who keeps a chopping block
covered with parsley jutting from his torso
to keep hisselves apart (his
lacerations supple signs of philosophy):

When the great urge to testify came
pushing in like white water from all the rooms
without central heating, and even the railroads,
Monsieur l'Ambassadeur wrapped himself in the blank gaze
of speechless childhood, and was carted off, the coward,
into the virgin pages of a hospital. His revolver
became soft and impotent, and the great hum
of truth that was in the world looking for means
of expression became the generalized din of consumption,
a Berlin wall of televisions, fridges, and stereos
blaring out tears, pent-up sighs, wordless senti-
mentality, and something like physical symptoms,
which the world appeared to be, to him, in him,
and to the watchers. All around him, the cardboard
body of a huge Stalin was growing out of all
proportion to the photographer focusing in on his
tiny head. The editors of night, those antlike
monks in charge of trimming night to reasonable size,
swarmed about the edges of the pulsing heart of cheap

43

newsprint and tore out long columns of lies where, shattered,
lay the good gossips with their smashed complaints.
Hate-filled stars, asterisks pulsing, literature
called for blood. A stud in hospital slippers,
he moved from switch to switch like a wobbly line
drawn by a drunk engineer around a body dumping ground,
turning off lights, turning on fans, setting off alarms,
tripping over the mad logs, his colleagues, calling
for certain features of heaven with swollen tongues,
until he found himself before an exalted light pouring
from a stained-glass window, a veritable orgy
of colored light lavished on his puny and emaciated
person, and behind him was a black wood altar containing
an embroidered towel in which something twitched, and
a big, great electric fish on a sculpted ceramic dish.
I'd like to be outside, he murmured, but there was
no more outside, only this great weight of religion,
this oppression of God, and he looked up. His eyes
rolled upwards out of him as effortlessly as if they were
two eggs of brown light lifted by a spring breeze,
and were lost in the darkness of the Gothic spire's needle
injecting the blue sky with sight. He poured
through his vision, or in his vision, which carried him
like a rickshaw, into the darkness of the tower,
and became a liquid. The liquid that was sight, and
presence, and which the Great Syringe used hoping
to get the skies to lift their great empty chambers,
where God used to live, and make way for another sky
where He might still reside. And all this with the poor,
bulging, tired, eyeballs of a hapless ambassador
from the provinces who one day, in fear of mortality,
nearly succumbed to the great buzzing bees of truth.
Write this down, it's me, the busboy said it.

Aye, but he tells the truth,

the maitre d' he sigh.

Under these circumstances
a little populism is in order,
and the Socialists are just the ones to give it to us,
a little relief for Chrissakes.
Enough of architecture, more planning please!
Indignant, the customer rose to put the bill
into the ballot box, murmuring loud enough for everybody:
*Dormir c'est souffler un peu.*

Dumb but true, like all things evacuated
by the very truth they claim.
Cryogenics or dogma. Laws or institutions.
Contagion. Pleasure. Violence. Commerce.
The equator. Extravagance. Alaska.
"Just as the glaciers increase," said
F. Nietzsche, our good friend, "when in
the equatorial regions the sun shines upon
the sea with greater force than hitherto,
so may a very strong and spreading spiritism
be a proof that somewhere or other
the force of feeling has grown most
extraordinarily." So I take a good look
around, and see that brother Nietzsche was
right, as usual. All around us threaded
through the full-time simulation of pleasure
in which the world is presently engaged,
run currents of spuming black arts, the pin-
points of death maps all over them, everything
overlaid with instructions and written in small
print, in filigree, and at certain angles,
and they are shuffled & reshuffled every second
by great paranoid Shakers with both their hands
firmly on the boards and on the flippers.

Come see Commander Monko at the Koinonia,
he's from another dimension, and with him
are a hundred transparent beings eating human
jam with their X-ray hands, and he stands half
in and half out of a large green egg shouting,
What is it? What? Quick! Lie! Stand up! Breathe!
I came here to see how the store is, who minds
the store, one, two, quick, give me your watch,
it's not gold, no good, breathe! One! Two! Quick!
In Seattle the gurus met a few years ago
to discuss the weather. Not good, they said.
Whereupon the volcanoes, and James Merrill, all
erupted, and Edgar Casey bought a piece of Virginia
where winds don't blow, and great shoots of pain & light,
a wire mesh of symbols, slipped like an underquilt
under many parts of speech, including nouns but
mostly adjectives. Which left only the verb people,
us, to shift for ourselves as best we could, dodging
the illusions of the insane mass, and their cabbages,
æsthetics, engineering, and embryos.

Engineers fix up the dried-up mug of the President
with beer. On another billboard
her thighs move slowly to engorge our willing selves.
A pall of sleep lies over us. Occasional violence
wakes up somebody to fun, fucking, fanfare, form,
the full five mintues of total squirming by which
the mess augments and rips things like cloth and materials,
silk and underpants and London Fogs. It's like
a turning upside down of Apollinaire's heart, to spill
all the love on us, *coeur renversé*, like fairy dust
or cocaine, forever, and with little golden lights in it,
light aphorisms for the abruptly airborne, and the slowly
rising. Dig it here, outside it's all but gone.
Funny how the butterfly Chuang-tzu, a reversible fragment,

insists on the prose of myth and will not,
under any circumstances, recover history for man.
Funny how he and other of angelic ilk get by
both the historical and the ideal, proceeding upwards
from this particular man here,
a horny bastard, lost the night entire,
having whiskey, mustard, cocaine, like I said, and great fountains
of words in Blarney's Bar, to the scattered applause
of two fat cops in drag revolving on their stools, over-
sized ballerinas at the Musée Grotesque. These are my
mustard brothers, he proclaims, and these my mustard
sisters, yielders of great big keys fitting the great big
doors of the decades, slammed shut upon the continually
retiring mustard seed of the soul, a firefly, in the dark
tower, with a book and a regret. The book, by Nerval,
flows like the neon above the tired square, nothing
but porn at this hour, and a limp chain or two over sweaty
leather. One can easily see Huncke here, and his Beat
friends, tourists, checking out the night in the interests
of literature, and Soviet critics bent on vodka. But mainly
he enjoys the particular eddy he creates, the swirling
thick mustard of fraternity, and the outside chance
that difference is yet in the world, enormous, if perilous,
and the clashing currents roaming the night may yet
proceed in the direction the twentieth-century *bohème* sketched
out for the collectors and the fools, a direction made
necessary by its being, alas, the only direction not leading
to the Camps and to the Army. *Le Paradis n'est pas
artificiel* but one must have an alternate hell, or go
with Mr. Lowry to the Farolito, or with Doubleday to
the remainder pit, not to mention Hitler & the rest.
There is no talking that does not lead to this, and to
little plays based on this, and the tap dancer jumped
on the table and made a great dance of this based on
the songs on the radio, eyes closed, feet beating the

47

Formica with the message that he was here, and he was
glad to be with us, and we were there too. It was a Morse
novel of feet calling and describing all of presence and
its necessity, a beat of forgetting and insistence
on the now, and a firm, albeit desperate, reiteration
of here as being here, I mean there then, here now.
The time has clearly passed for the partisans of now.
If they, we, want to make their, our, presence felt
we have to greatly beat our feet on the ground made
from the heads of our contemporaries filled with
oblivion gas or, worse, detailed visions of exactness,
maps of the very heads they describe *and* fill,
and then hope that the desperate beating in a prose
so beautiful as to wake the lit crit in every heart,
lying (alas!) disconnected from the gas-head at the feet
of some other entities with which we rarely if ever
converse, will reconnect head and heart thus causing
the layer immediately beneath (the great
ontological floor, O Mintho!) to, in its turn, begin
to beat its, their, feet on the heads of those below,
and so on, through all the many cavernlike interiors
of the baby cosmos, until exhausted, intoxicated,
and utterly ecstatic, it meets the Great Outdoors
and their symphonic No. Or Whatever. A real job,
if ever I get one.

The great discovery of my thirties is plurality.
Don't guffaw, Maurice, please listen now.
All my life, and that includes the half of it
which is distinctly literary, soon to surpass in sheer
numbers of years all other, I have thought,
along with babies, bishops, Copernicus, and Sartre,
that one's job in letters and in life
was to express a self attached to a head
which can then be detached, cut off, *tu sais*.

I tried to stumble my way out of the box of self
as best I could, given the orders I had, which
included complete directions to every museum
on the planet, but found myself creating monads,
perfectly selfish little globes of soap, not firm
like tits, nor smooth like spheres, horrid new
selves bent on conquering the gas stations for new
energy to propagate themselves concentrically
through life and lit and sometimes through the park.
Which is not, as I see it now, the point.
The point – put here your place names with Point –
is Plurality, Point Plurality, to be exact,
a landmark that's been here all along, on which
Mr. Jefferson grounded us and made us a building
at Monticello, in Virginia. Point Plurality, almost
exactly the way it is in Mr. Murdoch's papers,
and in these buildings from the days before
taxes, modesty, civic restraint and fake humility,
and the way all noble rhetoric would have it,
including my citizenship lecture and the loving
drunken bash afterwards, in other forms. In other
words, all other words, not just the tolerance
of difference, but the joyful welcoming of differences
into one's heart spread out like the pages
of a newspaper. The pursuit of the dialectic,
as Monsieur l'Ambassadeur would say, without which
one cannot live, although, alas, it is much harder
to practice in words than in the kitchen.

For you, I said.

He handed me back my arm.
Whereupon I grasped tightly my cliché and thin-lipped
went through the door into the street
where the small animals are barbecued.

I did enjoy the pale winter sun.
I made the most of the spring breeze that lifted minis.
I let my tongue wag into the summer heat and collected
a whole urn full of lovely sweat.
In the fall I fell with the leaves and was *désuet*.
Winter came to take me to bed.
Streets, cities, waiters, and parades —
these were the hair my various barbers chopped,
falling in great profusion into place, exactly
where they belonged or not. So using the conveyance
of the "I" to get us through the streets I came
to the exact meeting place of a thousand "I"s
clamoring for attention with an uninterrupted
belief in culture and the Pie.
I hovered there until I found you.

It was no ordinary party. Ted Berrigan was there.
Anselm too. And so were all the great orators of
our time and theirs, and a number of philosophers
in the corners, with that corned-beef look in their
deli eyes. And the music was LOUD! I mean,
we rocked! But for all that, you could hear
every word and our voices were nearly alien
to us because that unnaturally low or high pitch which
we acquired in order to talk above or below music
was nearly gone, and we spoke the way for thousands
of years people spoke, without the din
of perceptual cultural imperialism, but clearly
in the din of the market only, if we so chose.
I mean, when we wanted din we went to the market
and talked so the policeman wouldn't hear us.
The world is louder but the policemen listen better.
The old chickens squawking and the screaming gypsies
were as good as nature when we needed cover.
Like I say, we were both loud and clear

and happy knowing both schedules and eternity,
simultaneously upside down and horizontal
like bars on a music sheet in a big bed!
But there were some gents and gentians on the canopies
who looked as if they'd eaten the green apples of jealousy
and then OD'd on the wormy peaches of reason,
embarrassed recipients of large grants and prizes who
had removed themselves from human company.
One of these, a pathetic necrophiliac with spindly legs,
said that when the mind matures the sentences
come fully fleshed, in erect glory, and indeed
a full-fleshed sentence hung at half-mast from his sad
erection. It was *I paid for the gas so where am I?*
There are these bummers even in heaven, close even
to the mystery itself, not too close, of course, for
fear of being burned, but close enough. They sit or lounge
within sight of the mystery itself, scribbling on, not
seeing it. Once in a while they stop dead in their tracks
and wriggle as if the devil was in them. What happens is
that the mystery has a public-address system and it broad-
casts spontaneously and for fun, to blow their minds.
The mystery with in-built megaphone came thus to Lorca,
Mayakovski, Hikmet, and Ritsos, but not in translation.
Most times, however, the mystery whispers, depending
on attention for its erotic food, which it demands
without fail, to keep its flames fanned. "Our job," said
brother Blaga, "is not to uncover it but to increase
its mysteriousness." And so the mystery burns
giving off only enough light for the enormous job
of making oneself. Each time, every night, all
experience must be renewed. Others' successes or
failures are of no importance. The flames are not
bookish, and the sooner you give a child his or her wings
the sooner they'll get on with it, and that is how

from generation to generation the overprotected rich
get weaker, and overprotective tribes lose their sense
of hearing and their anger, and they begin to cater
to the dead. The dead lie like a heavy book cover
on us, our tombstone. It is their business to take
our time, to oppress us as much as they can, until
we say everything for them and train others to be dead.
They blackmail us every minute, so fuck them!
Must we always, like mad Swiss bankers, synchronize
what happened then to what happens now?
I'll write the poetry I always wanted to, or none at all.
The conventions of my generation, life, teachers,
lovers, maps, cars, music, art, the things I've said,
fuck 'em all, ploys clearly of the anxious dead!
The content that fills the flowing shapes
of my heart's pure yearning is communal like the city.
A fraudulent but real place like any other.
The infinite and the political do not exclude each other.
The particulars of a face need not break the concentration
of desire. *Au contraire*, they could augment it. And
in psychoanalysis and other therapies, people pay
for what they are missing, but not in order to recover it,
only to be confirmed in their lack, to be reassured
of the normality of absence, of the utter popularity of
the abyss, the sanctioned nothingness, the triviality
of death. Oh, we were vacated by the gods, they cry,
so we had to put language in the hole! Or waiters!
Well, I prefer the mask to the well-thought nothingness,
as I have said before, and I only took this job because
no one is doing it. The job always, the only job,
is to be an ontological reminder, a real pain in the
ass, reminding everyone why we took up the pen
in the first place, to scratch ourselves on the wall
or under the aching arm, to kick open the lid, to set

the water free, the hair loose, the spirit flowing.
Make you hear again that metarooster crowing!

After I had my soup a fat lobbyist, selling satellite
contracts to Indian and African businessmen at the next
table, took football jackets out of his satchel
and presented them to the grateful foreign nationals
who interrupted their scheming on how to get their
countries' treasuries to Switzerland, for a minute,
and said, The Raiders! Yeah! Yeah! We love the Raiders!
I interrupted my meditation and thought of Salvador
Dali, how it is possible to praise this world and
plunder it, without renouncing either others or the next.
I also gave a brief thought, because my curry was late,
to Kant's disciple Fichte, who said, "The Not-I is the
product of the I," a truly egocentric take needing
an instant Galileo. On the other hand, and here
I fiddled with my spoon, without the consciousness
illuminating the big It out there, how are we to see
it? By the neon of Chicago, natch! And then
the curry came, and it was hot, a red mountain atop
a purely golden bed of rice surrounded by little opal-green
islands of onion and mango chutney, and warm hissing
flat breads giving off air bubbles, and hope. The I
is neither product nor originator of the Not-I. That is
posing the problem falsely. The I is the enemy of
the Not-I, its colonizer, conqueror, and exploiter,
and here I dove into my food and was fierily gone.
The I is in the business of substance sucking, de-
sacralizing all the routes and getting fat.
The Unknown is my food, and that is that. I take
my rest at the Richmont Hotel and have my hair
groomed, and then I walk. There are
people who wish to show their solidarity with their

53

fellow creatures. Others want only to display
a spiritual difference. My company is with
the former but my sympathies with the latter. After
the light comes the odd turn, then the giant feather.
In the warm lobby I find the latest newspapers. I sigh
for Carmen at the cinema. Oh, close my word-weary mouth,
you arch, cross, vaulted, fleeing Gypsy slut!

# THE JUNIATA DIARY

# THE JUNIATA DIARY
## With Timely Repartees

Being a select menu from a variety of entries, in and around the time its author traveled on trains to Juniata College in Pennsylvania, a Mennonite institution of higher learning, the only place in the country to offer its students a Department of Peace Studies. There were other brief journeys during this time, notably one to Ann Arbor, Michigan. The Juniata River flows through the remarkable little town of Huntington, Pennsylvania, filled with trout. The windows of the little stores display fishing gear, guns, and sporting magazines. The house fronts are fancifully carved in several styles of Pennsylvania Dutch rococo. Just before the college, beside some ancient rails, there is a slope full of huge, multicolored plastic eggs that lie exposed transparently to the moonlight. This abandoned dinosaur hatchery belongs to the Corning factory, the town's only and rapidly decaying industry, which makes eggs from fiberglass to replace the bulkier metal tankers on the roads. They are very light, these eggs, and later, when I got to know my students better, we came here at night, crawled inside the glassy pastel embryos and rocked back and forth, attempting to roll down the mountain. Something of that rocking motion was put into this work. The other thing was the shadows: a person inside one of these eggs could throw a serious shadow all the way to the bottom of the hill over the rooftops. Several persons could create a giant shadow race to oppress the sleep of the town indefinitely.

The repartees came with the rewriting when the present insisted on talking back to the past.

10/24/79

Red Square's filled with people looking up
to the leader. Suddenly:

57

a sound like that of a field full of grass-
hoppers in August: a million
men are pulling down their zippers at once!

Don't do anything if the masses aren't watching.

2/11/84

Today as I type this on the KayPro 4
attempting a first real work,
Andropov of Russia dies, the Russians
are losing in the Winter Olympics at Sarajevo, where WW I
started, it is snowing in America & there are
a million men and women in Red
Square about to pull down their zippers.
I have the most erotic relation to the Fathers
of Communism: it was the backs of their bronze heads
that I saw contracting & expanding, drinking air
through bronze wrinkles
when my first love, Marinella,
took my scared bird in hand
in the Musuem of the Communist Party
and in the name of Marx, Engels, Lenin, Stalin & Gheorghiu Dej
released me from the prison of my adolescence
and from the drabness of the fifties. Together we set foot
into the sixties and the future.
That wonderful museum was to us what the hot leather
of your car's back seat was to you.
The frozen solemnity of the performance was enticing.
It wasn't rock 'n' roll but it wasn't death either.
"Don't do anything if the masses aren't watching"
is what we said then. The masses seemed eternally stretched
before the furrowed brows of the Fathers behind whose backs
we did our thing. Today when the masses *are* watching,
both the corpse and their lengthening shadow,
the bronze heads lie on their sides like their stone

58

predecessors on Easter Island and I feel
that my generation standing before the mausoleum
in Red Square is about to tug at their zippers,
to tug at the big zipper of history unzipping
the Nylon Curtain and the Leather Wall. Sheer nylon stockings
atop a leather jacket. Ah,
the prophetic powers once so miraculous seem only tawdry now
when the only things to prophesy are miserable things, in
and of themselves of great bitter value.
Only a fool would now be proud of being a seer.

10/25/79

Sleep linguistics. (Re: U. of the Future.)

Languages spoken in their sleep by the world's exiles.
Lost languages, surfacing only in sleep
where spouses and lovers can hear but not understand them.
They wash on the shores of our bodies these languages
full of the terrors and intimacies of childhood
things we swore we would forget but knew
that unless we abandoned, burned, eradicated the words
we never would. But languages have no place to go
but in – so they wait for us to go to sleep
and turn into monstrous novels filled with the complex
doings of the people we could have been
if we had never left.
At the U. of the Future, Professor Mayakovski
is discussing with Professor O'Hara
the pleasure of belonging somewhere. Still,
says one or the other, there is this matter of language
spoken in sleep. And the matter of belonging
taking root in dreams while the best of the next
five generations go away and speak no more. And would
you teach such sleep speech
and can you make it plain?

Utopia is a state of mumbled slumber.

59

The Japanese have sleeping parties at the beach, where
everyone takes Valium and sleeps on the sand for a minimum of
three days and three nights. Recorded, their dream language is a
peaceful drone, harmonious even. And the company says
it does the workers a world of good. As opposed to the
jagged fragments people hounded by police make in their sleep.
In the auditorium of sleep there is everything, from the monosyllabic
sweetness of young American girls at pajama parties to the roar
of men in strait jackets. I don't envy those whose job is to bug
our sleep.

10/25/79

A. on the bed: pants twisted around her ankles, shirt bunched
like an Elizabethan collar around her neck "expressing" her
tits thin geysers shoot past her ears into the Peruvian pillow
a drop lands on *The Pit* by Frank Norris, another on yours
truly who was once deprived and feels uneasy and so writes
buns in the air pen in hand. In the other room sleeps fitfully
the victim of the expressive carnage who is being weaned.
When he wakes as he does every half-hour he bangs his head
on the wall explaining the water Moses drew from the rock.
A.. "I have to do it, my tits are rocks."

2/11/84

The beneficiary of that paragraph, five years old now and
literate, with words and keyboards, speaks thus:
"I'm smarter than Einstein, Dracula, a policeman, and a doctor."
"Daddy, I love you.
Turn your face to me.
You are my enemy.
I am Luke Skywalker.
You are Darth Vader."

10/24/79

The eighties will be located at the psychointersections of cities,

60

where the schizolinguistic nodes form little flowers
of random anger & secret life: Narcissus &
Labyrinth, Gist & Pierce, Melville & Frisby, Bland & Winner,
Eastern & Fear, Fear & Market, Dolores & Market, Fifth &
Zeno, Perkins & Pliny, Broadway & I, Ovid & Stanley. The only
refuge from Yumpdom's Carlos & Charlies. The Halloweening
children, whose masks never come off, tow the cultural iceberg
to the windowless bank. Maddened daily columnists ride
atop the cute monads at the tops of buildings. Men like H. L.
Mencken and Herb Caen, heroes of the quick wound & the Don
Quixote stride, shooting walls of TVs as they pass. The cities
come back like sci-fi spores Blade Runner style.
Fire & the asbestos pyramid. Flesh & cement.
Social realism.

2/11/84

The eighties start properly now, in 1984.
A gun-metal tasting now. Licking their rifle butts
young Americans take up soldiering again.
The psychointersections of America now have
real psychos posted at them holding assault rifles
in one hand, croissants in the other.
I did a broadcast on them, they came from Main on Main
mainly, but were ready to stand guard.
Social realism would truly be interesting now (as there
isn't much now now) said Sam Beckett to Maxim Gorki,
because it would be facing the unbelievably
changed types and reality of no now now, a mind-boggling
challenge. Let's call for social realism, nay, naturalism à la
Huysmans (not à la New Yorker certainly), said Sam.
The result may be like early photography:
That can't be me! The total demise of the
abstract is finally at hand. The reporting of one's own news,
following the models of Huysmans, Pound, Williams, Olson, Kerouac,
Berrigan, Hollo, et al. – in a manner directly and combatively

61

opposed to the reporting by UPI, AP, et al. The Reuters of my day is clicking against the Reuters of They.

Let's not be so rush now, said Maxim.

10/24/79

Wanted for Semiotics Museum: incomprehensible signs. Signs from the minds of demented bureaucrats. Public notices. Supermarket signs. All signs pointing to something not intended by their maker. No art, please.

2/11/04

I began collecting these in Baltimore. Foreclosure signs. Notices of public nonhearings. The house became full of junk. Then I got in a newspaper fight with the Baltimore Museum of Art and all museums ("fronts for the art racket") and took all the junk and left it in the semiotic coatroom of the place. I gave the Museum my museum, in a surge of systemic generosity. Only the police was not amused. Periodically, we have these run-ins with Art. Painting WHAT'S THIS PIG THINKING ABOUT? THE TIME OF REVOLUTION IS NOW! on the back of the copy of Rodin's Thinker at the Detroit Art Institute. Collaborating in an immense sidewalk colored chalks cartoon lasting for five intersections and eight streets until it ended in a policeman's opinion of art: "I'd give my six-year-old daughter the switch for stuff like that!" (Detroit, 1967). Riding Benny Buffano's animals in San Francisco (1972). Collaging in restaurants, on sidewalks, at recitals, in bed, on tourist postcards. (Always.) Me & my friends we were the ancestors of graffiti art since the Altamira caves and before that we figured out a way to make the graffiti small & invented writing. Now we're fucking with the scale again, thanks to the Russian revolution & capitalism's endemic insanity of sign writing. Reading large things back into small type, and writing large to talk back, it's a job, lemme tell you,

62

and the art critics are pointing the wrong way on purpose. You read it here.

### 4/20/80

A fine intelligent girl who travels and possibly smokes and almost certainly always tosses her shoulder-length chestnut hair around after she speaks, took me (or was "I" her?) to the mouth of the mighty roaring waters of the river (the Delta) to a wide dam. The trip was free, unpremeditated and full of car crashes and big trucks going over cliffs and hitchhiking on mountain roads and doing whatever was right. The mouth of the river was a wide cement hole into which one of our enlightened companions stuck his head and refused to come out. We saw written on the stone below his body: HERE LIES DROWNED OF HIS OWN INABILITY TO QUIT SMOKING A BRILLIANT LAWYER AND AUTHOR. But eventually he came to & we — but not her & I — parted. She & I went on to the vast muddy plain on the edge of the sea where we saw a bum covered with sludge trudging through oil & industrial waste. "Why do you do it?" we ask. "Because I like it." At length he told us why he liked it, why pollution was *really* OK & we believed it. The dream ended upbeat. The dream itself was — in the dream — the greatest plot ever plotted. Car crashes, sludge, poisoned sources — a journey to the end of industreality.

### 2/12/84

According to Francis Crick (half of the DNA pair) as related by Tom Clark, dreams are the reject models of the diurnal that didn't work out. To remember them is to root in the garbage. Debunked by K. Rompf in *Exquisite Corpse*, Crick has yet one more debunker in this dream: a rejected model does not present itself as love amid sludge. If it does, the meaning is too painful: the abandonment of love for cleanliness. Or the equation of cigarettes with love.

*

# A BRIEF (REMEMBERED) *HISTOIRE* OF REJECTION

## THE TRICK

To make daylight. To put a mirror in front of the Thinker: to occasion Narcissus to meet the anus. To have them speak to each other (through the heap of junked structures in which they squat) in hermecholalic masomaneuvrable slang (*the hermetic/hermaphroditic echoing echo of what has been left out of language through the maneuvers/manipulations of the masosocial contract*). To reach into the sleep of the race for the forgotten, the rejected. To send the self (shaped as a bomb) into the shit pits. All the archlogs & archeologues of rejection to report to me by four. Over & over until no one shows up (in the dissolved heavens authority comes up over & over, and over & over form the rejected heavens). Society is the product of rejection. It is the form of what it doesn't want. Its borders are carved up by the weight & pressure of what it has thrown up/ squeezed/pushed/puked/killed. To dredge the outside back in. Dredgers to join diggers here by four o'clock. Dredgers to turn the glove inside out. Diggers to go down into the dream shit pits of the race.

## REJECTIONIST COSMOLOGY

In the beginning, a spaceship flew by. The alien astronaut, disgusted by the monotonous diet, threw his half-eaten sandwich down on the black rock they were passing over. The sandwich fell on the rocky blind orb and proliferated. Humanoid germs came out of it carrying little meat suitcases with Swiss stickers on them. Eventually — after the passing of many pullulating centuries known melodramatically as history — the germs began to remember their origins and to have ecstatic visions of their home in the alien sandwich. Slowly, in a concerted but unconscious effort, they commenced re-

turning to an original state of primal garbage. When they
were all buried in the waste products of their dream of Eternal
Return, they were seized by an inexplicable but perfectly
stupid sadness.

## TO REMEMBER

The politics of memory. The state of memory. The unre-
membered, the exiled, the banished. The citizens of the State
of Memory: Images of Success. Tito shaking hands with the
Yankee bandit. Stalin & Roosevelt carving floral meat lumps
on the map, their shoulders touching. Mother feeling good,
a rose in her teeth. Father away for a week, the town squares
abandoned to dream in. And outside? Outside memory? All
the alien organs, the undulating terror, the ejected Rejections.
Far in the Horizon (ten four, over) are the Great Rejections
looming up like the stones on Easter Island. The ancestors.
They are the Rejections involving more than 51 percent (con-
trolling interest). They have been exiled so that the body
(locus of shifting I's, beehive of I's waiting to swarm the
flowers...ah, Rose, your body is Jesu!) may survive. Weighted
down with Oblivion, pretty good stuff, eh? The Rejection of
Rejection.

# THE THREE BODIES OF OBLIVION

## I. DISBELIEF

Common, diurnal, regular, average, axial, knife-shaped,
shish-kebabed first body (weapon) in the three-word vocabu-
lary (arsenal) of Rejection of Rejection. He calls you "pig,"
and you must disbelieve. See all the victims of malfunction-
ing disbelief? Half-human, half-pig, they wallow in the plugs
in the Urbis & the Burbis. Good Functioning Disbelief, on
the other hand (with the other hand) takes the "pig" out of
quotation marks and makes it part of the little Rejectionist

Zoo each citizen ought to operate. There, the pig joins other scornful beasts, named after the animals we have exterminated, whose forms of being we have rejected: hyenas, imperialist dogs, dodos, turkeys, slimeballs, worms, ostriches with heads in sand, donkeys, parrots, snakes. It is a National Holiday and all the children are visiting the Inner Zoos, holding on to their parents' hands, prior to being rejected for looking.

WARNING: *Disbelief is nocturnally nonfunctional!* Literalism (dreams) takes its place. At night, you must push the pig through another door yet

### 2. LITERALISM (DREAMS)

Good news, folks. All those people considered lost over the years & under things have been found. They are in dreams. Turns out the dream's the greatest employer hereabouts. All the rejected – we just call 'em lost to go easy on you – have good jobs in dreams. There is only one job actually but everyone shares it: dredging. Dredging up, that is, to an ever-transparent surface the bodies of those who have dreamt themselves below all contact with language. Those statues on Easter Island are towers of language, grown enormous with the articulations of power. The power they need to pull out the bodies they are always about to pull out. The bodies they pull out are also pulling them in, with all their strength. Rejected themselves millennia ago (lily mollusks rainbow machines) they are rejecting (with all their might) the entreaties of transparency. What they mistake for entreaties (seduction) is actually brute force. The ancestors, both above and below, are very tired. Thus they are slow & often do no more than tug gently at each other & wish for Total Oblivion (the Three Bodies Thereof) to cause one or the other to float up or down. They half-dream themselves of others, lost in their dreams. A progressive paralysis invades the dreamer, flowing in like a wheel of lights.

66

## 3 . IMAGINATION/DEMIURGY/POESY/ INTERCHANGEABILITY

The mythical/collective/legendary incarnation of Oblivion. Vertical to Disbelief & Dreams which lie flat on the Diurnal & Nocturnal, balanced uneasily on a wavy line drawn by the drunk Mr. Hegel as he stumbles Home. So drunk he does not see the lamppost, vertical to the sidewalk he had trod so cheerily the other way only this morning, looming in front of him with the matter *dolorosa* of his brains about to be handed back to him. In this lamppost, shedding an imitation of day inside the German version of night, the two planes are reconciled, chewed up in an unrecognizable pulp by electricity, to look good & digestible for eventual reconciliation with consciousness itself. The chewed-up pulp of day & night we continue to improve on is going to – upon impact with Herr Hegel – affirm the Totality. My poesy, said the poet, as he helped the unconscious philosopher to his feet, is made up of the chewed, indigestible, unswallowable material of Rejection. So when the poetry itself is rejected (by guardians of the word cage guarded themselves by invisible censors with Shakti cattle prods), I am sent flying backward on the diurnal-nocturnal planes to reverse the gravitational axis, annulling, momentarily, *all* the Original Rejections. Affirming, in other words, the being forced to such deviousness. For a moment – in the rejection of my chewed-up rejections – I am made whole. My first reaction, enthused the poet, to the rejections of my poetic creations has always been one of extreme exhilaration. In that moment I stand affirmed. What I have to say – the doctored ancestors, the pinned cell, the dream amœba thrashing in the word net – has touched the limits of the world. I've come to the end of the world. To the end of what is known. *Au bout du monde.* Everything around the known world (the tiny, as in medieval geography blowfish world) is rejoicing at the arrival in the World (outside the Perception

Curtain) of a New Poetic Monster, a Dæmon, a New Substance. Livid vivid putrefacta. My creation, ah. Livid Vivid Putrefacta Rejecta. The poet threw his arms around the moon – dropping Mr. Hegel – and found himself embracing a cliché. Word garbage men picked up the sheets of paper flying behind the pair's uneasy progress Home.

4/24/80

Leather & Pampers: A White Bondage Book.
Heart of the Mall: A Teenage Hate Novel by Etta Monroe.

People-islands. "I know other people exist, but I don't know what they do." Or: "I know everything: whenever I don't know something, I ask myself a question & there it is." These people-islands, fertilized by huge birds way before the arrival of Cook, move among us sometimes. When we discover them, we put cheap condos on them.

Job: Mowing the Evergreen Lawn Cemetery.

Will used as a muscle. Will on automatic. Machine. Like language on its own. "I use language the way I use public transportation."

The island-muscles in the island-people meet the muscle-islands in the people-islands.

*

The glass prophylactic: eyeglasses.

Rock 'n' rye.

2/12/84

Eyeglasses, prophylactic for the eyes. So I won't make reality pregnant. Vision fertilizes reality. Between you & me, from now on, there better be a glass curtain, baby! We're too much together. *Journal d'un myope.*

5/23/80

The calisthenic cultivation of the will, cont. (Memoirs of a future cigarette quitter.)

The Healthy Abstract Body.

The Light Body is in the Physick Body is in the Abstract Body is in the Light Body.

In the sixties we cultivated the Light Body but found ourselves shipwrecked in the seventies on the Abstract Body, which we are now beginning to recover as a direct threat to the Physick Body — in other words, not applied morality but automatic extra brain.

*

I can't allow myself to be debilitated by health (he burst with repressed health: the fragments rained on heaven). All the vitamins dislocated his consciousness so that the dry, well-preserved body lay like a thin strip of jerky under the roving eye. Or: when the body overtook the borders that the mind laid upon it, the mind abandoned it to its own devices and watched it spread mindlessly like a puddle over everything: left alone the meat didn't know itself.

*

"What could an amnesiac nonhistorical and thus nonrepresentative politics be like?" (J. F. Lyotard).

Like Mary's Monte Rio farm on certain hot summer afternoons. Like inorganic one-of-a-kind lumps in certain immutable black holes. *Everything* repeats itself (i.e. remembers) in order to perpetuate itself. The refusal to perpetuate (to repeat) is the only amnesiac politics. Prehistory is, of course, amnesiac. In Eden (*illo tempore*) there is no need for memory. Whatever memory there is is unconscious, involuntary memory — definitely not political. Politics (the polis) involves consciousness, i.e. memory. In this world (the political one) Edenite = Sodomite.

69

History is the history of the organization of common interest against the chill of perception. Close the window, will ya. Give me the money & wait here. Buzzard cheese. Greyhound bus. Garage doors. Goering's diary. "*La loi de la valeur est désaffectée*" (J. F. Lyotard). The loin in the valley is disinfected.

Ah, for the "*motion's radical indifference to differentiating anxiety*" (Lottringer). Why are my hands shaking? "If you want to be one call this number." Cornelia says, Cinderella's is the story of a search for tight pussy. If the shoe fits. The mind's activity is health. What you perceive as English is Romanian spoken through a mask.

*

The physiology of translation. The body shaped by sound. Locuses: Throat: Slovak; Chest: Italian; Cortex: French; Neck: English; Wishbone: Persian; Hairline: Hungarian; Eyeball: Chinese. First, he spoke Throat Slovak, and she replied in Hairline Hungarian. This made him so happy that he wished her a good day in Wishbone Persian, and she surrendered to him in Eyeball Chinese. They wrote their vows in Neck English and vacationed in the South of France, where their innkeeper spoke Chest Italian.

The physiology compensates for the aftermaths of translation. I compensated for the loss of height incurred upon arrival in New York by grabbing onto a literary misunderstanding by which I pulled myself up those two feet I'd lost. Namely, I read "You're in the Pepsi Generation" in a subway as a line by Allen Ginsberg – which put the subway in *my* ball park – not as Ginsberg's source. "They may be taller here, but they are beholden to literature if they quote Ginsberg on the walls," I said to myself. The two feet regained were like the two feet lost – real & not real simultaneously.

Loudness. Loud languages (Spanish) drop to a whisper when the talk turns to illegal matters. Americans didn't use to care –

70

nowadays their voices drop uncharacteristically on buses and trains: a nation paralyzed by Something.

2/12/84

The waitress at Louie's Café came up to us and said, "Keep it down!" Yefim, who is a recent Russian émigré, started nodding OK, OK, no trouble. I started screaming, "*It's un-American! I can talk as fucking loud as I want to! It's un-American to be quiet!*" Jean-Jacques, a former friend of mine (as of this) was there, waiting in line to be seated. I spotted him as we were leaving in a great loud huff, and I exclaimed, "*Jean-Jacques! Look what the waiters are doing to us!*" He acted embarrassed, as if he didn't know me. "When the gods died in France," I told him, "they replaced them with waiters. The French worship waiters. *A nation of waiter worshipers! Servants of servants!*"

10/8/80

I love the abstracted way in which junkies make love.

12/3/80

I learn by osmosis & *débarass* myself of what I've learned quickly – the only wear on the wires (going hay bananas) is from mail, telephones, etc. (The active amnesiac seeks non-mechanical bride.)

12/21/80

Politeness = male flirtation. Manners (European) (insert phone call to mother) are the equivalent of women's conditioned come-ons. I come on so I have to go. I came on so I had to go. I smiled so I had to go. Go fuck. I came off the boat so let's come. I come on the boat so let's come.
*

*Mon index mesure le ratio de l'amour sur le tirage.*

### 1/12/81

Poetry-on-condoms parachuted on cities, the gradual abandonment of the vagina in favor of the asshole, increase in man-machine, woman-machine relations, food & air agents causing sterility, the inability to love – all these added to psychocryogenics are propelling 85 percent of my generation to IMB (Imminent Mental Breakdown). IBM = Imminence of Bored Matter. Flight of Styrofoam cups around a malfunctioning humming Xerox. Nostalgia. Nostalgia & the Machine.

### 2/10/84

The IMB theory neatly summed up what happened at the end of the seventies (1980-1984). But I didn't see that the energy released in the breakdown (with some wild and quietly institutionalized exceptions) would be so quickly absorbed by the logic of home computers. I type on a solid chunk of codified madness. The parenthesis (arms) of the mechanical (mathematical) mother. It stands to reason that IBM would absorb all its anagrams.

### 1/12/81

Rebegin the process of reacclimatization (Eskimo in Florida) of mind to the exigencies of thorgasm (thought emission).

"The vacuum is ideally the anterior space of all semiophany" (Barthes).

After language flows over it, desire needs to heal. Erosion by the waters of speech, blows from waves, nibbles of semantic fish on the buttocks, participled future-tensed spiders on nipples, long Latinate words wrapped around the neck, short Saxon ones stabbing the knees or short-collaring with spikes the ankles, barbaric Nordic consonants in the windpipe – metaphors dearticulating the damage. The metaphorical body brought to the aid of word victims. The image in Romanian is a way of talking. The linguistic code recognizes a previous reality. It pictures it as it invents it. Images are embedded in the language like anchovies in a pizza. The rest of the language is there to support its pictorial inventions.

2/12/84

Is all mental confusion linguistic confusion?

Lacan & Co. say yes. OK, here goes a little anecdote which supposes that it is: D., a Romanian psychiatrist, trained in Bucharest (where Freud is anathema) marries an American girl studying there, and she brings him to the States. He speaks perfect English when he comes and, being rather arrogant as well as young, assumes that he knows everything. But, sure enough, he understands nothing. People's gestures baffle him. Their body language doesn't go with the words. Girls misunderstand him. What's worse, his wife's family, a well-to-do Virginia tribe, treats him with terrible condescension, as when he fishes all the family goldfish out of the pond in the back and brings them to the main house for dinner, and they are all amused. Or when he mows the beautiful three-acre lawn with an antique sickle from the father's sickle collection. He gets a divorce. To forget her and all the other women he meets who, incomprehensibly, reject all his advances, particularly after he manifests at his most romantic extremes by reading them his collected poetry in English – he volunteers to work at a mental hospital. Here he is, ostensibly in his milieu, although he is not yet getting paid: he is studying for a degree which, combined with his Romanian diploma, should certify him to cure American lunatics. But at the mental hospital, which is one of the ritzier around, he is in even more trouble. The madmen, who (if the answer to the above question is yes) are in here mostly because of certain discrepancies between their language (reality) and the world (the others' language/reality), understand him even less than the so-called sane people who adhere at least *pro forma* to the con-

73

vention of words designating what they seemingly designate. He finds himself falling (very quickly!) in the crack, then the abyss that opens relentlessly between words, gestures, meanings, sounds, intonations. His other language, dormant but wounded to the quick, is waiting just for something like this to come steaming and hissing like a geyser through the audible (and growing louder) tear in the English-speaking fabric. It begins slowly, a word here and there, in the middle of a conversation with a madman (who, even if he reports it, would be only proof of the informer's madness), but then it begins to happen in conversations with nurses and the higher staff He will begin innocently asking for directions to a certain part of the building and there will be several Romanian words in his English question. These hissing intruders from the linguistic volcano brewing in him upset the people he talks to. Eventually (through mechanisms clearly visible to anyone in the profession) he is committed as a hopeless schizophrenic and disappears in that huge boiling pot that America keeps for the purpose in a secret place, a pot identical for all purposes with the official Melting Pot, but quite obviously not publicized.

I know this guy.

But now suppose that the answer to the question is no. Can there be madness without language? Are there mad amœbas? Of course, even amœbas have a language. The only things that have no language are things, and how can one conclude that a thing is mad? The maker (who has language) may be mad, but is the thing? No, quite clearly, the answer is yes.

*

Fear for my child is old fear of love since loving meant loss. It is me resisting myself on the basis of a pact made long ago. One of the *promesses éternelles* of childhood which cannot be broken, because its logic is infallible, having balanced & synthesized all the possible givens of that time. The crystalline beauty of a childhood pact: a haiku, a stream. To articulate (dissemble) it is impossible except linguistically since its world has disappeared, leaving behind only the coded version, the pact. If from this pact fear should later arise (miasma from a swamp) it is because its terms have rotted but its formal authority is undiminished. Ghost = form. Haunted by haiku, verses (Blake's), syllogisms – perfected nodes (lumps) of language flying through inner space like meteorites (*idées fixes* banging against the interior of the skull). "The imp of the perverse" (Poe) is what used to be called "ether," stellar debris, flotsam – at times also glue. "Upward movement toward matter…devout realism…conscious fantasy" (Barthes on Loyola, on Loyola's moving not toward concept or synthesis but through unraveled concept – articulation – to the concrete, to matter). "Before language, there was nothing but bodies and their images" (Bonald quoted by Barthes). Radical imperialism of the image. "There is a way, theologically, to clear the image 'through the customs': that is, to make it not the rung of a unitive ascent, but the unit of a language" (Barthes). Which is what Romanian (in the version I invented for metaphysical reasons) does, precisely.

2/12/84

This sub-rosa Romanian is so rabidly transcendental you have to hang on with both hands before you start speaking. Because once you start speaking you will lift off into *causerie*, soar with epigrams, dive with bon mots and rapidly disappear in chantlike sunset to the Region of Moan. Which is why, like Loyola the Jesuit, I had to invent not Magic Realism like the South Americans but Real Magic. Not Abstract Expressionism but Expressionist Abstract. In other words, not making ideas carnate but liberating the ideas from the meat. An idea, to a Romanian, is a thing to crack, like a piñata, to see what's inside. There is no such thing as a received idea in this country, or rather there is no such thing as an unexamined idea.

75

But, of course, this is a strictly individual matter, strictly opposed to the public mind, which is composed *entirely* of received ideas. If an idea is large, public and enforced by the police, it is assumed to be unworthy of examination, a bad idea and a comfortingly resolute enemy. The people (poets) are kept plenty busy, however, by the job of cracking other ideas, from which, Pandora-style, issue thousands of embodied delights. Southern Europeans are therefore the opposites of Southern Americans whom they embrace but never sideways, as the world turns (the Magic Realists being stylistic children of Faulkner: South Squared)

1/12/81

"I call intoxication of the spirit, that state in which bliss surpasses the possibilities glimpsed by desire" (Ruysbroeck).

"God is like an onion because he is good and makes you cry" (St. Sylvester).

*

Language as colonialism. Perceptual imperialism wedded to semiophany march across the unnamed body — or "to make neurotic" in the surrealist sense; unleash fantasy machine, populate being with images, populate earth with schizobeings (*imitatio dei*).

*

The militant logos vs. the reductive illumination. Or: the Judeo-Christian wipe out vs. the deobsessionalizing & sabotage of language in Zen. The monks I've made up are Jesuits gone over to Zen. The system exploded in laughter.

*

IMAGINARY BEINGS

At birth, an Imaginary Being is very much like a newly born Infant. But unlike the Infant, he grows not by being Fed but by being Spun. A solicitous mother will bring her Infant to the Age of Sex by constant Feeding. A creator will bring her Creature to the Age of Sex by constant Spinning. When a powerful Vortex is spun, the Imaginary Being releases another. Unfortunately, this kind of Vortex is achieved only in a culture where no one questions the morality of imagination.

Everyone has, at one time or another, pricked a yogi with a needle and watched the sperm come out. But this is where most folks stop. In trying to populate the world with Imaginary Beings, most people fail, and many should not attempt it at all. Most of you are only capable of populating the world with a single being which is half-handed to you by your parents, with the other half culled from hypnogogic impressions. This is as it should be because not many can risk losing their minds at the hands of the two Fears: flying & public opinion. Public opinion has always been against Imaginary Beings of all sorts but never as much as it is today in America. The first order of business today is the elimination of imagination for the total protection of the Single-Identity Person. Anyone possessing more than one identity is immediately thrown in a hospital where they sever the "weaker" ones. In most of these cases, of course, the stupidity of doctors eliminates the original identity while releasing the Imaginary Being, and thus Imaginary Beings survive *vole volente*.

But one day, in the heat of persecution, a pall will descend over the persecutors, grinding the reductive technology to a halt. The fossil fuels have run out and "realistic self-appraisal" has become suddenly bankrupt. At that time, the few of us who have patiently invented and stored Imaginary Beings, either inside of us or in secret attics and cellars, will have something of a tremendous advantage, an advantage I propose we seize in revolutionary fashion to put a whole new set of fantasies in the myth basket of the race.

1/25/81
The nets are out, perfectly fanned, unavoidable. Calm sea,

bountiful harvest moon. Moray eels, surf fish, sea carp, tiny shark — all edible, bounteous, possible. A TV fisherman looks at the sunrise through Polaroid binoculars. This is the Chesapeake Bay filling my dream.

Later, she & I take the long & twisted roads in the old city, making out on parapets leaning over mossy cemeteries sloping into the sea below, my prick in her hand or her mouth, my hand in her pants or round her buttock like waiting to make a basket with the luscious ball, almost caught once by a venomous biddy in a vegetable camion, our eventual goal a trailer in the surf where her husband and my wife wait for us.

*

Business has skimpy records. Mechanization, coming out of the rationalistic tail end of theologian-philosophers (Nicolas Oresme) through Descartes on to nineteenth century, drives wedge between thought and feeling (Siegfried Gidieon). Tom Veitch's "psychic TV" as re-integrator. TV's TV. Alec shows me silicone panels of computer: the chips are so small with their printed circuits they would be lost if not housed in "huge houses" of plastic. Royalty. Miniaturization doesn't necessarily mean simplification (Walker) because the machinery needed to make the small, apparently simple, components gets bigger. The reactors doing subatomics have been getting bigger. The haiku factory is in a skyscraper. Millions of clear steamlined miniatures issue from the lumbering hulk of Corp corps.

2/13/84

Alice dreams that a box in the approximate shape of this computer, filled with some kind of books, arrives, emanating an odd radioactive light. The four of us who touch it are suddenly shooting jets of blood from our eyes. So she crosses herself and shrinks from the Devil.

I dream that I have stolen a pair of Shimanbaghi shoes, the latest, most expensive Japanese luxury objects in the world.

They are large square objects with curled tips (like short skis)
lined in felt outside and silk inside, and they have hundreds
of pockets in and out. I steal them in broad daylight from the
five-and-dime by pretending to make a fuss over a girl I am
taking outside with no intention to kiss whatsoever. Later I
stand from my dream and exclaim, *Caffeine doesn't access eter-
nity*!

These shoes are not shoes: they are computers. Which are
lining the pockets of my shoes for a first-class escape. The
two faces of the Devil in our side-by-side dreams.

### 3/6/81, AMTRAK

Bridges with empty niches waiting for rural madonnas.
Subjects of somebody's nostalgia. Not mine.
The backs of old Pennsylvania towns. Rusted boats.
Rococo iron grille. Car garbage. The beginning
of the century. The fantasies of children watching
from those windows. The new house backs are the saddest
of them all. A solar-paneled condo. Silos. Dutch
paintings. Cows. Tykes with waving kites. Old
church roof like ruffled nun's headdress. Black
flying saucers on the fields: the hats of Amish
farmers behind six-horse ploughs. There is a woman
in one of these houses with their backs to the train
who exposes herself to the 5:29 from Chicago but
the glare of the sun in the window blinds us and we
don't see her. She has her orgasm at 5:31 on the dot
just as the linkage on the last wagon flashes by.
She's been satisfied this way for twenty-one years. Her
husband doesn't mind. Old rusted disconnected rails
right by our side like Morse code. Displaced
consciousness like suddenly seeing your head next to
yourself. Hospitals high on hills. Closer to God
I suppose. Françoise Nicole Depuis liked the train.
From it she saw a lonely stretch of road in lovely

79

pasture country. There there she thought I will open
the best French restaurant in America. Françoise
is the daughter of Master Chef Depuis whose cooking
rated so many stars the Michelin gave him his own
Crab Nebula. At ten she had been drilled in Brillat-
Savarin & at fifteen she easily outcooked her father.
The little clapboard shack Françoise acquired was
an easy fifty miles from the nearest town in the heart
of Amish country, people notorious for liking only
their own food. Françoise hung up a sign that said:
FRENCH RESTAURANT, Françoise N. Depuis, PROPRIETOR
and then she waited, waited, waited, waited, twisting
now her starched apron, now the lace of her slip that
showed and showed. A week later the J. C. Penney salesman
working that country entered. She made duck *orange*
from personally caught duck, steak *au poivre* with
pepper brought by her father from the Côte d'Ivoire,
two soups, one sad and one happy, i.e. one that made one
weep and one that made one silly, a bisque, and for dessert
a torte, seven éclairs, and two napoleons.
The man ate everything. He thanked her. That was
nearly three months ago. Françoise is waiting. Won't
you help out little Françoise? The backs of charred
factories. Oily ponds with lotus blossoms on them.
Mercury water. Tufted islands in the Susquehanna
River. The four towers of Three Mile Island. A farm
house right next to it. And another. Cows. Sheep.
The "Art on Reactors" program of the National Endowment
for the Arts has painters and sculptors in the area
painting & sculpting grotesque masks, Aztec, African,
Egyptian, Soviet, Granadan, Cuban, Jewish, & American
to be affixed to the outside of the warm cooling towers,
to make them the true objects of cult horror we know
them to be. Death gods. Serial billboards run along
the highway running along the tracks. God in

installments. AFTER LIFE WHAT? A mile farther: DEATH.
A mile more: AND THEN? In one more mile:
THE JUDGEMENT. I note that everyone who is not going
to Chicago stands now, and they are wearing thick
belts painted with the Stations of the Cross. Silos.
Rich pastures. Silence. The fat Yugoslav conductor
steps forward with a radio, and the fat setting sun
blares forth from it. Beauty, it blurts, hurts. Beauty
hurts because it's subject to instant nostalgia.

## 3/7/81

Wake up in snow fairyland: mountain ridges in front of win-
dow, & fat flakes still furiously coming down. From my
dream, a slogan: Mylar for democracy.

✻

In the student-union men's room: "Beware of gay limbo
dancers."

## 3/11/81

The walls ooze an impoverished substance. The life chintz
of ersatz studentdom. My floor, which is my neighbors' ceil-
ing, shakes with middle-of-the-road rock 'n' thud. I will
have to make music war: my speakers against theirs (all war
being that).

Student prison. Jail. Siberia. College dorm. (The Pink Pal-
ace, a.k.a. The Pink Phallus, but I hear no phallus worship.
Only rock.)

The base guitar demolishes the house brick by brick.

The NEA is punishing me for talking back. (But what is that
compared to eternal punishment?)

Alone in an empty room in a howling college dorm. I think
I'll just go upstairs & say to the first person I see, Do you want
to fuck?

✻

The small honcho became very depressed when he came eye to eye with the big frog. The water level in the pond fell one hundred feet in ten seconds. The wind filled the absence as the amœbas vacated the water drops. (Fable of the Academic Hallway, late twentieth-century genre; see also Parable of Tenure, Garbled Minutes, Saga of the Chair.)

*

Rock 'n' roll has succeeded: their brains are Jell-O. Amusing tales are told (on my frayed rug) of property destruction, car accidents, fraud (registering a nonexistent student and grad-uating him in due course), epic puke-and-bash parties, survived drug overdoses. The cheerful anarchy of youth in the womb. I nod in ecstatic approval, cringing all the while at the lack of social "content" to the seemingly random bang-bash. I mean, in the name of the Revolution, OK. But smash a hand-carved chair just because it's *there*? The worst, they say, were the alumni of '73. Those guys! When they left the dorms, after the reunion, not a closet was left standing, not a drape hanging, not a window unbroken. Those guys! The original Animal House generation! I mean, you couldn't *make* speakers big enough for those guys! Their ears wouldn't *deal* with less than volume setting 10. My most enthusiastic anarchy fans are two cherub-faced hockey players who may even be virgins. The girls generally listen to these stories, nodding blissfully but noncommittally. What guys! they say when the guys glance in their direction. What yum-yum fools, when they glance at each other. They all smell like milk and tennis rackets and new skates, and all they want from life is "a good job," money, to be left alone (with everybody there).

*

"You know you're getting old when the girls' mothers look better to you" (Mark H.).

*

In the snack bar, by the pies, stands an armed policeman.

*

82

"Thank you for your humor," says he. As if "humor" was a thing like "cheese" or "first aid." Sure way to sour someone: turn their light into a thing. That being the problem with the saurkraut Fourierism of that Mafia matriarchy in Washington, D.C., The Finders. While they go on deliberately switching roles & studying each other to better vampirize the weaker ones. The obsessive quantification of light in order for the quantifiers to acquire what is surely the true future currency: humor, light, wit, spontaneity, generosity. They have money & they know money isn't *it* so they use it to free light by quantifiable degrees. (India? Akron, Ohio? Spin the globe! Our friends in the ELV await.) Future capitalism: the gerontocracy accumulates psychic currency (new currency) from youth floated by money (old currency). The world is being prepared for this new monetarism. We are going from the paper standard to the psychic standard. The reorganization of production & information is done for this. The etherealization of the exchange value, the thinning of the currency, the alchemy that turns gold to light through paper. (Circuitry is printed; print is electronic.) The only problem: capital, storage. How do you amass psychic currency? At this point, the people indulging in the future are those who can gorge themselves with the new value on the spot. Storage: books, records, videotapes, RAM & ROM.

2/14/84

When I expressed, as I often do, my desire for a printing machine, friend Deborah said, "The Finders have one they want to get rid of." "Terrific," says I, "when do we pick it up?" Next day: "They would like to meet you." "Meet me?" "So they'll know who has it." OK. So we go to Washington and meet two formidable women in their fifties sitting around a kitchen table in an elegant D.C. mansion by a vast park. Swirling around them are all sorts of men taking orders, carrying out orders, performing tasks. There are several computer terminals around. So we are introduced, and they ask me, and I say that I'm Romanian. "Romanian, Romanian…" muses the senior leader, "don't we know a Romanian?" The other one puts down the leg of lamb she's rubbing with coarse black pepper, and pecks at the computer keyboard. Stuff comes on the screen. "Two," she says, "we know two. One is a specialist in Turanians, the other works for Kissinger's office." "Good," says the Boss, "which one do you want to see?" "Neither," I say. "It's no trouble really. We just give him a call and he comes over. What are Turanians anyway?" "Short, mean guys on horses," I say. "Really, I'm here for the press…" "Oh, yeah," she says, "that's David's turf. *David!*" There is a commotion under the floor and up pops an elderly gentleman. "He's the founder," whispers Deborah. "He used to be in the CIA, then he founded the DCIA…" "Divine Central Intelligence," explains the cook. "We have no secrets." David is only too happy to fill us in. The Finders are a matriarchal community where the "strong" women hold sway over "weak" men. The two in the kitchen are the "strongest," ruling equally over "weaker" women and "weak" men. And then we take the tour: the top floor is where the women live. It is a big loft divided by flower pots, little bookcases, art objects, into small sleeping areas. The floor below is also a loft but it is much sparser and rougher. There are bunks, and no room dividers are allowed. This is where the men live. "What's the story on couples?" I ask. "Don't got them," says the Boss. "When a woman feels the pull, she calls one of the men up." "Don't the same men get called over and over?" I venture. "Yep," she says tersely. "Is that fair?" "Nope," she says, "but if they wanna get called, they should make themselves more attractive." There is a small theater where the group practices psychodrama, with the women leading. And then they take us to the inner sanctum, the war room, which is a round chamber with couches along the walls. In the middle of the room is an immense globe. "This," says the man from the DCIA, "is where we decide to go." He gives the big globe a spin, and the continents in relief, the mountains, and the seas spin. "Every month we come here and spin the globe. Barbara puts her finger on it and says, you go here, you go here." What they do, it turns out, is send themselves to odd parts of the world with no money. When they leave, their instructions read, "Go to Ceylon, come back with two thousand dollars." The men and the women go on separate trips. They never mix. The purpose of the Finders is to "acquire skills." They all know hundreds of things: carpentry, fur trapping, harvesting olives, word processing. "We catered Reagan's inauguration at the White House," says Barbara. "You could have poisoned everybody," I say. But they don't smile. They are not (seemingly not) political. Their experiment is strictly with role reversal and community. It all sounds pretty great, until I get back to the subject of the printing machine, and then Barbara says, "We'll network so you can do some jobs for us to pay for it." "I thought it was free..." I gave Deborah an evil look. "It is. Only thing we ask for is service." The other thing they do, it turns out, is "networking." Everyone, from Romanian specialists on Turanians to aspiring publishers, ends in their computers, ready for "service." "We are the biggest network queens in D.C.," says Boss Barbara. "OK," I say, "when can I pick it up?" "Soon." Well. We go back to Baltimore. Two days later, there is a knock at the door, and thirteen (!) rather hefty ladies of all ages are at the door. Barbara is with them. "We've come to serve," she says. "Your roof needs fixing? Your sink leak? Need baby-sitters? Want an orgasm?" "No," says Alice. They come in for coffee. They perch in corners, under the eaves, on the dormer windows. They spend the night. In the morning, the brigade is already up in the kitchen, boiling coffee for five hundred. "After coffee," I say, "good-bye!" "But," says B. the Boss, "we have a two-week mission in Baltimore. We have to earn six hundred dollars and establish a Finders' center." "Good luck," I say. And I haven't seen them, or their machine, since.

85

## 2/16/84

Among the kinds of power, the main ones are the power of the strong over the weak and the power of the free over the unfree, which coincide at most points except at their ascetic/monastic/beat periphery. There, freedom is detached from money (i.e. the way the society of the strong welcomes their own). To divorce desire from any object is not an operation for everyone. But it is the only way without La Revolución, which topples the orders & starts the bad news all over, with a different cast.

※

Being an outsider is not a misfortune, it is a blessing and, what's more, a script for freedom. It's not the suffering that's good for you, but the *thinking*. Thinking is impossible inside, where everything serious has already been thought for you by others. By the dead Founders. By the dead. Escape first of all the oppression of the dead, their blackmail. But must you synchronize the understanding of what happened then with what happens now? Possible method: When the past is terse and aphoristic, make the present anecdotal. When the past is anecdotal, make the present oracular. Ahem.

## 3/12/81

There is a fucking hole in this generation's motor: they're stalled. They're fucking Europeans or something. "We're more like Europeans now. We just don't trust anybody in power" (my favorite hockey player). "We're more like zombies now: we trust everybody in power with everything we've got" is more like it.

＊

The way the second hand caresses the hollow number (Timex).

＊

A way of speaking never tires of itself. But will we tire of it

86

when its fascination with itself overwhelms its fascination with us?

*

Racism is resentment at growing fat.

*

The fag barrier: the last small-town fear.

*

"They screwed me on the lettuce. Later, I got three heads for a dollar" (A & P).

*

The Spartan phalange/phalanx: dick power. Four naked men with swords back to back with hard-ons. Ready for anything. They enter the Italian restaurant & the customers pull the checkered tablecloths over their heads & dive under the tables.

*

Guilt is the envy of next day's smaller man.

*

When you're fucking a Rothschild & the phone rings do you say, Not now, I'm in the middle of a Rothschild?

4/3/81, ANNN ARBOR
Many Terry Pattens & Ron Padgetts around here.

*

Breasts enormous
   have returned
      with Reagan

*

Fat books
Fat boobs

*

R. R. shot on TV. There is a clump of students watching in the lobby at the Residential College. The mild-mannered young man I've just seen "about poetry" jumps suddenly out of his mild skin and screams: "*I can't believe he missed! I can't believe he missed!*" Reagan staggers into the limo under a wall of security and says, "What's his beef?" I say, "Woe!" The expert TV watchers: "No commercials?" When the NBC surgeon-in-residence says, "They made a six-inch cut in his side," a voice in the crowd says, "Cut!" And others take up the chant: "*Cut! Cut!*" Budget cut/TV cut. Today's children are satellites of TV planets.

*

It's spring! Sudden T-storm. Flowers. Bare flesh. Yum.
The shaking off of generalized dread.
Like a general delousing himself at the end of a campaign.
Like a wet dog.
Like a healing metaphor.

O great healing healthy metaphor whose shining flank
bumped the great diseased first term & sent it flying!
O great healing metaphor invented by my first exiled self in Nueva York
in the great year 1966 when the whole world was a disease
only the brilliant metaphor of my young body could heal
as it hurtled through Nirvana Village and Central Park open
like a gold sieve to the wonder of possibility!
(The only thing I asked is that it be intelligent possibility:
intelligence, a kind of cleanliness, a sanity certificate.)

It went like this, this theory:
suppose that you're in the presence of Disease, Obsession, Violence, Bureaucracy, Theft.
Each one of these things is but the First Term.
Suppose a patch of leprosy the size of a triangular stamp from Liechtenstein is growing on your arm and you are too poor for medicine and do not speak the native tongue enough to ask someone to lick it away for you. Why, then you must find the Healthy Second Term, and quickly – just as I just found it! Your cure: that stamp from Liechtenstein!

88

I rolled through my new country healing first my ills with poetry, than others', until at last a shaman, I stood looking at the two oceans simultaneously and knew beyond the shadow of a doubt that I invented it all, just as I made myself.

2/16/84

Eternity is not accessible through caffeine, his note said. But he needed a cup of coffee. Caffeine does not access eternity, said his computer, which didn't.

\*

A Policeman (Interrogator, Inquisitor): Time is a searchlight: it bathes you momentarily in brilliance, then darkness engulfs you. The rest is just fumble and try to recall. You might as well spill the beans.

4/4/81

Speech will make it well.

\*

Creative disorder/impatience. Things rushing in/out. Style designed for easy transport through self — we are holey. Things at an angle: autographs on the old serrated photographs my mother reproduced endlessly for provincials and soldiers with their heads sticking out of cardboard generals and ruffle-clad picnickers of *La Belle Epoque* whose dresses would have sufficed to cover hundreds of those goose-pimpled, bare-kneed girls of the late forties in that sad and rainy corner of Southern Europe. Things at an angle, in flight position. Serrated edges through outmoded bodies. Serrated/corrugated/ruffled.

\*

Knowledge as glue
　　Info as horses
　　　　wanting to be glue
Info at top speed

89

```
rides through the holes
   in youth
      continuously
         increasing speed
until it gluifies
         & seals the person's
            momentary self
            shut —
```

At first
   euphoria
then

      nausea.

The nausea barrier — as in peyote, gene loop, the DNA stair, knots, Bach, rococo — and the Other Side (reachable through the loop, stair, repetition). Or: Sleep, kids, sleep, there ain't no bogeyman. Without the "other side" there is no apparent end to nausea. But appearance being what it is, which is to say all that is, there is no end. The stair is infinite, only the nude continuously descends it: an acrobat descending a huge steel question mark. Proliferating form creates illusion of substance/thickness. There is no zelf & no nauzea, Herr Doktor.

Yes, master, I sit down on pillow now with Brother Veitch.

*

At college I speak against goodness. In bed at home I speak for love. My words throw my body against other bodies. Other bodies are thrown around by my words. My words toss bodies around as if they were coins in a boulevardier's hand. My words relieve bodies of their gravity — caused by their own flow of words — and toss them around wordless and speechless or full of remembered speech. Next morning the bodies thrown around by my words try to sneak back among their own words and are — rejected! Quick, more words for

90

the bodies rejected by words! But I have no more words, I am empty, the magician's make-up is smeared, the skin is old, culture cries in the emptiness. These bodies, taken out of their own rhythms, tossed about by my words, shut out of their own speech & out of their own rooms, penniless, jobless, without an automatic life, startled out of habit, jolted out of comfort, thrown out of paradise — these bodies must now change their speech, commit violence on their language in order to be taken back into the flow of language. The aftermath of every seduction is the murder of an old language. Along with everything *organized* (dearticulated) I am an assassin — at every level of harmony I am programed for destruction. When the flow of language — public composed of privates — transports the bather to heaven, I am released like Señor Earthquake, Sir Tidal Wave, & I engulf, penetrate, and annihilate — a job I invented for myself out of history. On the other hand, I don't have to put up with it — I quit smoke, no — so I sit on the loop-the-loop & watch the convolute exhaust itself. I'm probably one of those Tibetan monsters by now.

*

The Healing Metaphor (1966) in another way. Or how the Fantastic, Healthy term cures the Diseased First Term: if the First Term of my habitual paradigm is always "borrowed" (read/seen/imposed/linguistic/schizolinguistic, a chunk of autonomous psychospeech reaching for life/reality) it must of necessity be *weaker* than an outside term, introduced arbitrarily, fantastically, cruelly. The First Term is cultural, the Second is found anywhere. The healing goal is to eliminate the cultural First Term (including the "image" repetitions: self parodying self) and to move entirely to direct perception of the "outside." Be outside, go outside. It's spring. The "made up," the "formerly metaphorical" grows with attention. The quality of attention increases as you come into the orbit of the "outside." Methodological problem: I am used to digging up the imaginary by means of the cultural. (European Illness: TB. The Grand Sanatorium.) Solution: go directly to the imaginary (or the "truly observed") and allow forms to emerge as they please. Caution: forms emerging as they please may just deliver you to the sneaky rhythms of the *désuet* cultural unfamiliarity, one of the numerous sneaky disguises of the First Term.

History: in 1967, I was experimenting with all sorts of looseness, riffing, rhythm. (I had a different accent every day.) Then I tightened up a bit for my masters, the publishers. First, Paul Carroll raised my capitals & raped my text with punctuation. Then Mike Braziller with his insistence on the elegiac. Then my surrealist fans with their insistence on recognition (i.e. orthodoxy). All of these insistences, even when strenuously or successfully resisted, left some of their fingerprints, if not the shape of their pressure, on my work. Of course, one evolves that way too, nobody's a frozen CB. The question is only: Was the pressure to tighten the right pressure? (Pressure *is* pressure to tighten. Even when it's pressure to loosen as in massage or love. I pressured her until she screamed. The local mutant laughed, revealing a horse's head.) The pressure paradox. S/M. B/D. There is no paradox (transport) without metaphor. After going from the cultural to the experienced, from s/S to S/s, I realize that's an old fucking point. I'm just a fucking commie hopelessly addicted to dialectics. On the other hand, being "totally outside" gives me claustrophobia, like walking my burro slowly between the canyon (paradox) walls & thinking, Where do they start shooting from?

4/10/81

Ted Berrigan visit. Ted is a medieval lamplighter, a walking lamppost, a 3-D Tarot card. "The Gulf Stream of consciousness" (A. Hollo). He goes on through your brain turning on lights that've been out for years in rooms empty that long. The night watchman putting the light stick to Europe's first gas lamps. And he does it *talking*.

## 2/17/84

Ted died on July 4, 1983. Like the great American he was. He is a constant subject for meditation. His influence on me has been continuous since 1967. He was a father, as I've said elsewhere. At the time of his death I was beginning to forget him. Twice I'd been to New York and not gone to see him. This forgetfulness may have been true of others as well. By dying, Ted kept himself from sliding into oblivion. Christ died for the same reason: so that his teaching would remain fresh. When they say, "He died for you," they mean, He died so you won't forget. In that sense, Ted died the death of the great, just as a chieftain should. It was typical of his sense of humor that he died on the Fourth of July. But he didn't die without resentments. He resented being forgotten or ignored or miscast, and he continued resenting it after he died. I felt his presence several times, bearing down with fury (not out of my guilt) on me. Luckily, I have other dead friends (who have been dead longer) who restrained him and showed him the light and dignity of his new position. And possibly the reason for his death. Likewise, Christ didn't die forgiving enough. The jagged edge of his resentment is covered in sectarian and fanatical blood. It cannot be denied that the great die appropriately (it is part of their greatness), but few of them let go of the world easily. Because of it, the world goes on fighting their battles, but without greatness. The shabby and the mediocre battle on. There should be a course at the Great University to teach the dead to let go of this world easily, with rancor.

## 4/10/81, AMCHAKA CHAKA

If you can divide your eyesight between a tan skinny blonde stretching to get a box from the luggage rack and the tufted islands in the middle of the Susquehanna, you are learning to see like a seasoned traveler.

*

Layered flirtation: an older lady goes by & incredibly, she is flirting. It is a layered flirtation that says, I want you to dig not only *me* but *my times* as well. Say Caruso & she expires with pleasure. Culture is the aging of flirtation, the skin surrounding the core of desire, the plea to commune horizontally first through history, then through the body. In fact, as the body gets more frail, the cultural envelope becomes dearer. In very old flirts there is no body offered at all. Old flirts beg you only to kiss the little finger of their times, if you can find it. In death the flirtatious disappear only when no one can be found to give the nod to culture — this sometimes years after the body's gone. Ghosts are shapes of unconfirmed desire. The old flirts are desperate survivors of their bodies. They are the agents of a culture's last attempt to be understood. In them, the *esprit du temps* truly dies. I smile back but she has gone.

*

My mother is an old flirt.

*

The heartbreak of exile is the (temporary) inability to flirt.

*

The Jews, a flirtatious race.

4/12/81, JUNIATA

I like people with horrendous romantic illusions informed by the embarrassment of them to pay total attention to the particular — even if only to discredit it. The particular observed in this fashion is doomed, tragic, strung along by entropy, passing, time. Death, apocalypse, the end of time illuminate their reality retroactively, shining backwards through things on their way to the impossible. Dreams desire themselves

94

into being only in dreamers forced to become natural scientists by the huge embarrassment of reality. Dreams come true when death lights them up from the wrong end of the viewing glass. Dream lit up by death = concretion. Demiurgy = employment of death by dream. Eschatology = scaffolding. Employment = disciplined energy. Energy disciplined by form = particular. People with horrendous romantic illusions, in love with death, I want to go to bed with you! I want the gustatory thrill of the embarrassment that wavers thinly – Greek shadow play – between you & total snuff. The need, born of embarrassment, to *prove* the insubstantiality of things is the source of all discovery & the object of all my desire.

\*

Through my open windows
      the screams of virgins
           on the dorm beaches

\*

Pat here belongs to a Death Row Support Group. She's been corresponding with a "beautiful man" on Florida's death row for a year. "What did he do?" "I don't know. He ran off with the circus when he was fourteen & then one night his feelings got the better of him." "Have you read Genêt?" "No. But I've studied the way he is going to die. Horrible!"

\*

*Le rest est style* – a drop of sperm on the end of my stylus.

\*

Mifflin, Pennsylvania.

\*

Tactic for now: Total Inappropriate Simulation (TIS). Go to faculty party dressed as student. You are neither. Minutes later order everyone to hand up the wallets. Go to shop in beach clothes. Go to beach in coat and tails. The pursuit of inappropriateness (the right to). Stanley's DOOC (pronounced

95

DUKE) movement: Dress Out Of Character. The deep-cover
bandidos today are in totally inappropriate situations. Inap-
propriate simulation on death row. An innocent man on the
electric chair, reading a book.

### 4/4/81, AMTRAK PSEUDOSONNETS

Honesty is the hardest thing to fake.
So say the actors sincerely.
He spoke American punctuated with little explosions of joy
in foreign lingos.
Congenital optic mimesis: vulva mouth speaks to *cojones* eyeballs.
We've come all this way to acquire the right distance:
at first we were both
inside & outside then congenital mimetic optic fragments
began to walk away with our images inside them.
See? These are some of the broken leashes held by the bank.
After we walked away we planned to stay out but it seems
that our selves walked back inside & something else
walked away with us & it is getting dark.
One trillion acts of violence were committed on TV last year,
all in the dark. One violent act for every dollar of national debt.
Years ahead of Big Macs sold.
The race for infinity is on
but if three people are flying together it's not so bad.

\*

I see a building called PERMUTIT in bold ebony black.
I think, I made myself a peculiar niche in American lit.
Perlmutter used to be my name, fallen angel my vocation.
Permutit, pearl mother, wanderer, pearl nipple, Jew tit.
Roving tit, migrant mother, vagabond breast, nipple bum.
Boob on the lam, rotating UFO, fleshpot on the warpaths.
I am heading toward you, both of me, on the 4:15 trains.
I come from both directions, from Chicago and from D.C. &
I wonder what does PERMUTIT make in real life and am I

96

then in the *Fortune* 500 & what's the stock quote for Friday?
*

It's non sequitur to the non sequitur of chatter, but it's sequitur most sequitur to the great Converse, Senator Señor.
*

The literature of mobile homes, trailer parks, squatter burbs, sub-suburbs, living in parks, where is the literature of the exhausted roving of America? All those beach ends in Florida, the carved-out bits of National Parks, wild on the maps but crowded like Calcutta in reality? Where are my sonnets and my odes to the folk who just went through the bottom of the sieve and were not heard of again, who found the places where roads don't go, where planes don't fly? Where are the founding epics of those whole countries that rolled under the table when the high stakes game went on between white men with guns and Indians with pipes? Where are all those nations of the divorced going off? I mean, instead of following roads paid for by taxes and remembered on maps, how about following the trails of serial numbers on cheap department-store stereos, following their myriad little red lights into the bewildering wilderness of nowhere, or trying to account for every car, its history, its demise, and its final place of rest? By their objects you shall know them, they said, and they moved directly into apocalypse & delusion, the horrors of moving. They faced each other hanging from the rolling figures ploughing all under until nothing was left. Not their names, certainly. Except in the memory of unhappy nieces, cranky old uncles.
*

I don't take any chances, said the postal clerk checking his ID. That's why you're an old lady, the old man said.
*

She addressed him weirdly, in the fifth person plural. "You are both sleeping," she says to her husband, including herself

97

in that "you." "The second person schizophrenic?" he inquires.

Your own voice answers your call from somebody else's telephone-answering machine: it is the fourth person singular.

God on the phone: the Sixth ($3 \times 2$) Person Possessed.

Chicken knees talk to you from your plate: it is the digestive second *intime*.

Yugoslav train conductors fattened by microwave sandwiches & bribes address each other in the Amana formal eighth.

Pronouns are holes or handicaps in golf.

You must write a novel in the second person plural schizophrenic & tape-to-tape fifth. It is called *Echoes of Gravity*.

Chapman, the assassin, is *no man, chap man* is the zero degree of the pronoun.

Between the plural third & the proper name stretches the vast zone of the zero degree of the pronoun, a swampy region teeming with the virtual & the dead. This is where the compost of language and the as-yet-unborn lexicons fester and bubble in anticipatory proliferation. Up to my neck in muck I feel for erectile tissue in the warm goo and find my Turanian pseudoancestors riding through my grandchildren like silicone chips through hothouse breasts – but softer of course and mud to the touch. The reason Madman Lit 101 is often so boring is that it wants desperately to be understood where it would suffice to note the phenomena for the madman's                                     private use. Much vision destroyed by madmen's exaggerated ideas of its value!

Value is a fixed pronoun. When it tries to draw a bead on the swarm, it turns into the surrealist who doesn't go anywhere without his party card. Value is the first person singular at anchor.

*

98

Three teenage hoodlums in the club car are undoing a fat girl with their lust: she'll fuck them all before the journey's done. Ah, trains filled with lust & thought or both! The two fake ballet dancers going to the remote Romanian provinces in their hasty uniforms: they began dancing before we even pulled out of the station. First with the conductor, who forgave them their lack of tickets, one after the other, then with me, as if to flush the fat conductor out of their bodies with my sixteen-year-old virgin body. And the Gypsy sleeping in the luggage rack who came down in the middle of the night and covered me with hair and secret musk. The rhythm of the train is the rhythm of sex and thought, as Blaise Cendrars knew, because both are the joy of the expanded heart, the plentifully oxygenated blood.

4/21/81, AMTRAK

Tolerance is a most un-European idea. Pedro the Mex says, "In Spanish we have two words for *liberty*: *libertad* and *libertinaje*." "In Engamerican," I say, "we have hundreds: *liberty, freedom, license, freakdom, liberation, loosening, taking it easy, easing up, letting go, relaxing,* and the specific forms: *hanging out, wipe out, blowout, flying, nodding out, blissing, dropping in/out, satori, orgoning, digging it.* The Mexes are babes in the woods when it comes to ze deliberate pursuit of liberty. There are whole *catalogues of liberty,* Pedro! We have supermarkets of liberty here, amigo! We even borrowed yours: we have a special shelf for *brujos* and their boom-boom!" "Eh," says Pedro, "this is just more crime." I admit it. Europeans, Latin Americans, they are civilized people. A grid of manners stands between them and experimental liberty. (But only when they are at home: here, out of the grid, some of them become very criminal and/or artistic indeed.) Not until an *entire* society breathes for a minimum of five minutes a *collective criminal air,* can they even begin. *Norteamericanos* are *synchronized* to crime. We suck it into our lungs collectively every

99

five minutes for at least five minutes. The burning shards of terror left in the lungs & the heady carbonated rush to the head hurl the populace in search of liberty. Or death. The speed & the crassness nauseate your basic Euro-Spaniard who would rather make revolution.

### 4/22/81, JUNIATA

The sad saga of Barry Kramer. When I first met him in Detroit in 1966, he was rich and sad. Everything he applied himself to turned to gold. He lived in a house with a bank vault the size of an apartment. He asked me if I wanted to investigate, and when I said OK, he locked me in there. I heard him turning the big metal wheel, and then everything was quiet, metallic, claustrophobic. Terrifying. Like the dream I had of all the clean metal graves of the French poets in Père Lachaise. I knocked on the door and the walls, beat my fists on them, but I made no sound. How long does he think that I want to be in here? I thought. I mean, how long is one supposed to experience the marvels of entombment? How long does he think that *I* want to experience this? I was terrified to suddenly have to reassure myself that Kramer was a well-meaning fellow. Just because he was rich. He'd hired me, hadn't he, an unemployable foreigner, in his Mixed Media store on Cass, a room full of hippie paraphernalia and books, and I had run his store with great aplomb, often closing up during the peak hours of the evening to take a skinny black lesbian or a barefoot flower child to the basement, there to give them a choice of cultured boxes to lie on: "Fiction? Or science fiction?" Invariably, they chose science fiction. That's the kind of times those were. And he had fired me, it's true, for neglecting the business, but I remembered no bitter parting, no mean words. So how long would he keep me in there? After all, what was I to him? And the only two reasons I had come up to see him at all were (a) he was always in the company of two beautiful black fashion models, and (b) he had good drugs. But what if he was asking himself the very same question? Why did I come to see him? These were paranoid times, especially perilous for a rich hippie child whose money, capable of buying guns and drugs, must have been a definite threat to the police. And the police *was* everywhere in those days. With a little help from grass paranoia there was as much police as blades of grass. So what seemed like eternity passed and the big door stayed shut. At last, there was a clanging in hell, and the light and Barry Kramer and a cloud of smoke entered the grave. He handed me the marijuana stogy, and I sucked gratefully, with an eye to the crack. But suddenly he shut the big door behind him and said, "I told Laurie to let us out after we smoke this." And there we were. "Why can't we smoke out there?" I ventured. "The smoke can't escape from here. No place to go." So I closed my eyes and sat on the round metal floor with my back on the curved wall and sucked in the smoke. What I knew about Laurie wasn't reassuring. Word had it that she had been a great model once but that since meeting Kramer, she'd become a spaced-out flake with a razor blade always handy near her anorexic wrists. What was reasonable paranoia before became a trembling mountain of dark foreboding. Of course, Laurie had the perfect opportunity now to leave us in here forever. It was her chance to make a clean breast of it. And the more I smoked, the more I was certain that this was the realistic version. What's worse, I couldn't stand Kramer's proximity: it was vaguely sexual in the most threatening way. Just me and you and the metal, baby, his way of handing me the joint said. Laurie let us out, and I never went back. Kramer started *Creem*, a magazine for junior rockers. He bought a radio station. The wilder his ventures, the more money he made. He made the gritty Detroit sound nationally famous. He died in his bank vault, from an overdose of nitrous oxide, presumably laughing himself to death.

*

A student tells me that the latest rage on campus is plastic trash bags filled with nitrous oxide that people put over their heads. Only, two nights ago, they removed someone's bag to find the someone blue, cold, and dead.

There must be something in our culture that makes people want to laugh to death.

8/12/80

## A PETITE HISTOIRE OF RED FASCISM
### (for M. Brownstein)

All connections
are made by energy.
The inert masses
know nobody & not
themselves. Nobody &
Not Self are well worth
knowing but connecting
them takes energy
so they are known
only by their masks
of inert proletarian
matter   Bolshevik
statues. The people
with the most energy
employ themselves to
know the statues. The
statues are well-known
by the inert masses.
The people with just
a little less energy
are then employed
to interrogate the inert
proletariat. One energy
grade below, the police &

mental-health apparatus
employ themselves to
energize the inert mass
which is now for the
first time broken up
into individuals.
Breaking it up releases
energy – enough energy
to respond to questioning.
The police level then ex-
tracts a primitive narra-
tive from the recently
inert & this narrative
generates enough energy
& excitement to produce
a two-level discourse which
makes sense to the upper
energy level. New
energy is created & soon
the top echelons are
introduced to the dis-
courses of Nobody &
Not Self. Together,
the brass & the mass
envision the statues:
the energy of the mass
will henceforth be em-
ployed to make statues
of the brass.

3/8/81, JUNIATA

PORTRAIT OF A COLLEGE

A Gogolian G. S. manager bites the ends off cigars
   has sign behind him says THINK

The student body is pimply floral it can use
    three pitchers of water to cool off
I'm sure the bookstore clerk is queer
    first thing he says is *My wife says no*
The pipe-smoking theologian keeps a Bible in his gym
    locker has on striped shorts
Bells ring ten minutes to the hour the dogs salivate
    on the Formica and the enamel
In the old campus building an athlete on crutches
    leaps forth chugging grape soda
That siding company keeps calling to fix your
    house a secretary tells the fat provost
I won four Dodger tickets from WKRZ for knowing three pitchers
    who pitched one hundred hundred-percent games
The plump disco body of overfed rural America
    says don't fuck me now I'm on a diet
After I turned into a couch I became a hostage
    to the distending of my person
The mystery of his existence eluded him so he turned
    up the stereo and died
In the primal laziness and solitude only the salad
    made crunchy little noises
High schools full of this body! Junior colleges & Bible-
    belt colleges full of it!
But the anorexics & hemophiliacs are at Yale & Harvard
    beaten thin like rugs for five generations
A new study says people were thirty feet tall in the time
    of Moses he just walked in the sea
Another new study says God made rocks & plants seem older
    than they are to test our faith
The Mormon missionaries were nice shy boys & we fed them
    but didn't agree so they walked back
God behaves like a savage in this one instance
    & the bells you hear are on tape
The student leads a life without memory &

is working toward a degree in oblivion
I read your article & I must say it is amusing total
    nonsense don't you know
You are uncouth enough not to take full advantage
    of my person so bug off boy
I exhort the paymaster not to deduct taxes he is
    dipped in oil & unctuous gray
At the train station a cheerful & slippery man
    extends a chalky hand I shake
I buried everyone in these parts for forty years
    he says I went to business school
His four daughters sit on the bursting suitcases
    & chew gum by the tracks
The knit powder-blue sweater on the eldest pops
    & two .22-bullet-sized nipples burst forth
The jeans on the youngest give out at the seam
    & her fresh white ass cantaloupes into view
The others slide off the croc valises lift their skirts
    & pee on the terrain
The blue mountains & the green river dream around them
    like shell-shocked recruits
I'm a mortician's wife mom says and I've seen them
    come & go & I'm from Philly
The college on the hill & the prison on the ridge
    keep this town from going under.

## 3/9/81

Mark's News Store on the corner: fishing tackle & guns. The
.22s start at around forty dollars. I would get me one, go into
the old Penn Hotel next door, sit at the polished wood bar,
order a shot & some fries, and be on top of it. Instead, I go
into the old Penn Hotel here, sit at the polished bar with the
four midget Elvis dolls, order a shot, & look around politely.
The boots of the unarmed man pinch him. What a rich coun-
try America used to be: art-nouveau mirrors, curving stair-

ways, & everyone ready to fire. *Towers, open fire!* The bar *is* vast: a bowling lane. The flannel-shirt crowd, I mean the *old* flannel-shirt crowd is dispersed along the curve of the bar like an open-fan boat attack on Venice. In the watery mirrors. The lively midget waitress waltzes along the polished coast to inaudible rhythms with bottles of Gennessee beer. "Play a song, woncha?" she flutes to an old drunk Viking and flips him a quarter. After an hour at the jukebox he comes up with "The Yellow Rose of Texas" and "The Green, Green Grass of Home," and when he makes it to the bar, proud of his color coordination, the waitress says, "A quarter sure ain't what it used to be."

*

Politics, says El Stiffo, is the struggle of individual temperamental differences for control of the social arena. He is a cook, generalizing from the politics of food.

## 8/14/80

Certain things of extreme importance are only toys which have
        come to life.
Gasoline truck, "pipeline on wheels," can circle the planet
        nonstop eighteen times.
Our field trip to the ugliest part of New Jersey included
        boiling book vats.
The best books in America are boiled here including
        his own the teacher said.
A gray gluey vapor formed a big cloud on top of them called
        James Joyce and Company.
This pen's so new it squeaks like a gumshoe on a black glass
        sidewalk.
Three-pronged masterpieces made a mesh of tunnels in the Hearst
        empire.
Ugly blows like beauty persecuting the girl in the paper dress
        & her nude boy.

The baby-sitter is the baby's first agent she mediates
    its reality & is mean.
Frozen at reentry we were taught to perform the mechanical
    tasks of manners.
Irruption of underdeveloped old psyches in the absence
    of the Bay Bridge.
The muted sexuality of silent trees falling in the mossy forest
    fills us.
*Je suis le pont entre les amoureux et les bureaus qu'ils*
    *échappent.* I am
The bridge between more rocks & the desk drawers they've escaped
    from. The better
You talk the wider the divide. That's the other
    shore if I'm correct.
In preparation for monkhood he doused the raw cauliflower
    with curry & salsa.
A new language made partly from words thrashing in the net
    wanting to go back in the water.
Baby-sitters, tourists, travel maps, sunglasses, tanning
    lotion, pimps, shirts.
Invisible agents masquerading as words walk through
    the doors of the Ritz.
Psychology of unrequited hysteria once it was grapes
    now it is sour grapes.
I would love to put my virgule in her verge never mind
    the raisins this is love.
The blood spots on your résumé made us think
    that you are the one & now get!

8/14/80
Turns out
    everyone
        turns out
obsessed with the line upset with the line
    they get in line

it's too straight     it goes straight on out     it doesn't stop     it's
                    U-turns all the way
          we toe it
                but we don't like it
          so I bend it for them
                & I empty it
          or most of it spills
                    on the grade &
          the curved track
at heart we all play with trains not ride
          Is everyone happy?
                You got your crab apple
                    you won't miss the mango OK
but no
          they graft & concentrate & do botany
          they turn the crab apple into
                a pear
                    the pear
                          into an orange
                the orange
                    into a grapefruit
                the grapefruit
                          into a melon
                          the melon
                into a mango
                          They are there
                    *Paradiso!*
                The branch is laden with mangoes
                it's straight
                mangoes on a line

     *

A railroad man on flying: "I would drink likker if I could
drink likker. When it goes off & when it comes down, that's
when I pray!"


108

Besides all their other sins for which they will surely fry in
hell surely, the big-house editors in N.Y.C. have been doing
violence to writers' chronologies. Things written at the same
time, linked by subtlety of atmosphere & *esprit du temps*, are
busted, interrupted, violated by sporadic publication, the
crass editing. Time jumbles, strained connections, impotent
rage are the new textures of works emerging into print after
years of neglect. The new things are mostly like the new
writers, things molded to conform. The new American writer
is a timid soul, a solicitous academic or a terrified lackey.

*

The *effect* of art is well-known by now: quantifiable/verifia-
ble/checkable/programable. It is known by tone, timbre, and
feel. It is what sounds "natural" to the graduate ear. The
graduate ear, the bourgeois ear, yawn, yawn, in the walls of
Now. The sensation itself of art is not disagreeable in its fa-
miliarity (it is *taught*, alas!), a civilized low-voltage charge we
know how to expect & where. The warmth of a new kitsch.
The low voltage of art now stands in marked contrast to the
high voltage of drugs. Here is the rub: art must define itself
chemically if it is to *deliver* (in both senses of the word). Its
low/quantifiable/recognizable charge can increase and shine
in relation to its history but it is irrelevant if it can't operate
at the highest levels of consciousness which are now chemi-
cally induced. An argument can be made for high conscious-
ness needing to be *filled* but even so you don't fill chocolate
éclairs with sauerkraut, or pralines with Lysol. I mean you
do (one does) periodically and when you're high, in order to
populate your divinity with junk, until you can't take your
own bad taste anymore & deny your divine self in total disgust
at yourself—which is the only way to come down. Gods die
of chintz, not forgetfulness. They're smothered in tokens of
sentiment. Early plastic, *art moderne*, pop-top tops & black
velvet three layers thick on Byzantium.

2/27/84

Devastated by revelations of innocence, the cunning old fox looked amazed at his perverse productions.

\*

Museums – the central tombs of our civilization, meant to allay the fears of the spiritually illiterate. The real job: to make all ye hear again that metarooster crowing! I only take up the critic's job to be an ontological reminder, to keep us (me) from forgetting the reason why we took up the art in the first place.

Composition in Ehrhardt by Walker & Swenson. Designed by Allan Kornblum. This book was printed on acid-free paper at Inter-Collegiate Press, and was sewn in signatures to ensure durability.